vegan

in association with the Vegan Society

Tony Weston and Yvonne Bishop

hamlyn

First published in Great Britain in 2004 by
Hamlyn, a division of Octopus Publishing Group Ltd
2–4 Heron Quays, London E14 4JP

ISBN 0 600 61190 6

A CIP catalog record for this book is available from the British Library

Printed and bound in China

10 9 8 7 6 5 4 3 2 1

Distributed in the United States and Canada by
Sterling Publishing Co., Inc.
387 Park Avenue South
New York, NY 10016-8810

Ovens should be preheated to the specified temperature. If using a fan-assisted
oven, follow the manufacturer's instructions for adjusting the time and temperature.
Grills should also be preheated.

Fresh herbs should be used unless otherwise stated. If unavailable, use dried herbs
as an alternative but halve the quantities stated.

Pepper should be freshly ground unless otherwise specified.

A few recipes include nuts and nut derivatives. Anyone with a known nut allergy
must avoid these.

This book is registered with the Vegan Society. Nothing printed should be construed to
be Vegan Society policy unless so stated. Any views or opinions presented are solely
those of the authors and do not necessarily represent those of the Vegan Society.

The Vegan Society
Donald Watson House
7 Battle Road
St Leonards on Sea
East Sussex
TN37 7AA
United Kingdom
Telephone: 0845 4588244
Fax: 01424 717064

www.vegansociety.com

contents

introduction

Like many people, you're probably eating rather differently from the way you did as a child: less meat, more fruits and vegetables, lower fat, sugar and salt. Maybe you've even cut meat and fish out of your diet and are already vegetarian. Perhaps you're now wondering what else you can do to avoid animal products and avoid contributing toward the wasteful use of the world's resources.

Wherever you currently stand in your food philosophy, this book is for you. Tony Weston, a vegan for many years, and Yvonne Bishop BSc Dip ION MBANT, a nutrition therapist, have compiled a selection of their favorite recipes and invite you to try a delicious cuisine that will almost certainly surprise you in its variety and taste. Banish thoughts of tired nut roasts and predictable vegetable stir-fries. Here you will find newly available ingredients, such as chlorella algae and quinoa, alongside old favorites, such as tofu and carob, to push the boundaries of vegan cuisine as never before. The authors gently dispel any misconceptions you might have that veganism involves tyrannical self-denial and prove that vegan food can be everything you want – delicious, attractive, healthy and full of choices.

Starting with a section of basic recipes that includes some of the staples essential to the vegan repertoire, the book is then divided into four main sections – breakfasts, light meals, main meals and desserts. As you'll quickly discover, the pleasures of good food without animal products are quite real and easily achievable. Imagine a day that starts with Chocolate Croissants or Creamy Mushrooms on Toast, moves on to a lunch of Asparagus Pancakes or Apricot, Beetroot and Cumin Soup, then finishes with Chestnut Cottage Pies or Arame Almond Risotto, followed by Date Toffee and Quinoa Custard Pie or Date and Dried Plum Brownies.

There are recipes for every occasion, from simple snacks to sophisticated dinner dishes, allowing for the fact that some days you have more time than others. You will also find quick fixes to hunger pangs, as well as our top ten sandwich ideas – all part of helping you to break the habit of skipping meals and relying on fast food and take out to fill the gaps.

Worried that vegan food might not supply enough nutrients to keep you healthy, energetic and alert? Just consult the section dealing with vitamins and minerals (see pages 8–10) to find out what you need and how a varied vegan diet can supply it. Any possible shortfalls are pointed out, and ways of compensating are suggested).

Far from being difficult and extreme, veganism is easy, straightforward and delicious – a great way to achieve optimum health and a clearer conscience.

what is veganism?

The philosophy of veganism is far from new, and many religions teach a reverence for life and compassion for living things.

The Greek philosopher Pythagoras (c.569–c.475 BC) taught the virtue of eating without causing suffering; those who followed the vegetarianism he espoused were known as Pythagoreans. Some 2,000 years later Leonardo da Vinci predicted, "The time will come when men such as I will look upon the murder of animals as they now look on the murder of men." Whatever your reasons for cutting animal products out of your life, it is a decision you will never regret.

The Vegan Society

Less than 100 years after the UK Vegetarian Society was formed in 1847, the ethics of consuming dairy products were being hotly debated. An attempt to establish a non-dairy group within the Vegetarian Society was rejected, so in 1944, a member named Donald Watson (b. 1910) was moved to act. He coined a new name for the non-dairy philosophy, announcing, "...vegan is the beginning and end of vegetarian." The Vegan Society was founded in November 1944.

The Vegan Society is a charity bound by its constitution to educate, provide information and promote ways of living free from animal products for the benefit of people, animals and the environment. Veganism seeks "to exclude all forms of exploitation of, and cruelty to, animals for food, clothing or any other purpose." In brief, it makes no sense to exploit animals for food: everything we need for good health and happiness can be found without using animal-based products. There are now vegan societies in countries all over the world, numerous books have been published under its auspices, and the Vegan Society trademark of authenticity can be seen on thousands of products.

Suitable for...

Unlike many other food products, those labeled "suitable for vegans" are actually suitable for nearly everyone. They meet the needs of those avoiding certain meats for religious reasons; of those cutting down on saturated fat; of those who suffer dietary intolerances; and, of course, of those who are vegetarian.

As manufacturers increasingly tap into the vegan market with its millions of adherents, so they add to the range of vegan products available. The variety is now so impressive – and so widely available – that shoppers of all dietary persuasions are as likely to buy vegan products as the non-vegan varieties, simply because they are delicious, versatile and nutritious.

The Animal Free Shopper, the Vegan Society's shopping guide, gets bigger and better with every edition; you can even buy vegan condoms, cameras and shoes. Vegans are a growing market, and manufacturers take their needs very seriously.

Everybody's doing it

Increasing numbers of people are realizing the potential of veganism and recognizing that it has become easier and more delicious than ever to follow. Research shows that most of us would prefer to be kinder to people, animals and the environment, and would do so in our shopping habits if it were always possible to choose an ethically produced item over one that might, for example, use child labor. Veganism is the solution to pleasing everyone, to being inclusive rather than exclusive.

Even if you are vegan for only 50 percent of the time, your actions combine with those of others to make a real difference to the planet. Don't view making the change as one big leap that requires 100 percent commitment. Do as much as you feel comfortable with and everyone will reap the rewards.

are you getting enough?

A balanced vegan diet can provide all the nutrients needed for a healthy body; even B12 (essential to protect your nervous system and heart health), which is found mainly in meat and other animal products, can now be obtained from fortified foods or supplements. Just as important is to get the right balance of omega-6 fats (from grains) and omega-3 fats (from plants and seeds).

PROTEINS

Proteins are vital for growth and repair and for regulating most body functions. They include enzymes (to help metabolism), hormones (to send chemical messages) and antibodies (to boost the immune system). Proteins are made in the body by different combinations of amino acid building blocks.

Some plant foods, such as amaranth, buckwheat, quinoa and soy, have all the essential amino acids, so are often referred to as "complete" proteins. However, complete

proteins can also be made in the body as long as all the essential amino acids are obtained from the diet in a 48-hour period.

Examples of complete protein combinations include:
• Grains or nuts with legumes
• Rice or millet with vegetables
• Vegetables with mushrooms
• Vegetables with sesame seeds or Brazil nuts
Protein requirements depend on age and activity and increase during pregnancy and lactation. The ideal average protein intake for an adult is about 20 percent of the daily food intake. A varied vegan diet can easily provide this. Protein-rich foods include pulses (peas, lentils, beans and bean products, such as tofu and tempeh), pseudo-grains (amaranth, buckwheat, quinoa), nuts and seeds.

CARBOHYDRATES

Carbohydrates – sugars and fiber – are the body's main fuel providers. The best are complex carbohydrates, found in unrefined foods such as wholegrain bread and pasta, brown rice and fruits and vegetables. Their fiber and nutrient content remains intact, so their energy is released slowly and steadily. This is far preferable to the rapid and fleeting highs provided by refined carbohydrates, such as white bread, white pasta, white rice, and foods high in sugar. Although fiber is not an energy source as such, it benefits the body by supporting the digestive system and helping to eliminate wastes and toxins, and keeping energy levels consistent.

THE VEGAN BALANCE OF GOOD HEALTH

(Calories obtained from food)

• Carbohydrates from fruit and vegetables 50%
• Carbohydrates from grains 15%
• Protein 20%
• Total fat 15%
  (of which a minimum of essential fats 5%)

The ideal average carbohydrate intake for an adult on a vegan diet is around 65 percent, with 50 percent of that coming from fruit and vegetables and 15 percent from whole grains.

FATS

Fats are rich sources of energy, flavor and fat-soluble vitamins; they help us to feel satisfied after eating, provide insulation to keep us warm, and help protect internal organs. They also play a role in many body processes.

Dietary fats can be divided into two main groups: saturated and unsaturated. Those derived from animals tend to be saturated and usually hard; those derived from plants (except coconut and palm oils) are mainly unsaturated and liquid at room temperature. An excessive amount of saturated fat in the diet can be harmful, as it leads to raised cholesterol levels, which can be deposited in the arteries and increase the risk of heart disease. Saturated fat can also block the body's conversion of essential fat; as extra saturated fat is not needed by the body, it is best avoided.

Unsaturated fats include monounsaturates, for example, olive oil and rapeseed oil, and polyunsaturates, such as sunflower oil and corn oil. Polyunsaturates contain a number of essential fats: particularly important are omega-3 (soy, walnut, rapeseed, hemp and flax) and omega-6 (sunflower and sesame seeds). These fats have a range of functions, including maintenance of the nervous system, the skin and brain function, and the balance of hormones. They are especially important during pregnancy and lactation.

Unsaturated fats are sometimes treated with hydrogen by the food industry to stabilize and harden them, a process that turns them into solid trans fats. These are even more damaging to the body than saturated fats, creating a greater risk of heart disease. Try to avoid them by not eating refined foods.

Saturated fat is sometimes recommended for cooking purposes because it is stable at high temperatures. However, olive oil makes a good substitute, provided it is not heated until it begins to smoke.

Vegan diets are generally beneficially low in saturated fats and high in essential omega-6. However, they can be undesirably low in omega-3 fats unless compensatory steps are taken. Flax or linseed oil is a rich source of omega-3 and can help to give you the desirable 3:1 ratio of omega-6 to omega-3.

Conversion of essential fats within the body also requires other nutrients to be present. These are vitamins B3, B6, biotin and C, and the minerals calcium, magnesium and zinc.

MAIN FOOD GROUPS AT A GLANCE

PROTEIN

Essential for: growth and repair, regulation of most body functions via enzymes, hormones, neurotransmitters and immune cells.

Ideal percentage of diet: 20 percent
Complete proteins: quinoa, amaranth, buckwheat and soybeans
Complete protein combinations: grains or nuts with legumes; rice or millet with vegetables; vegetables with mushrooms; vegetables with sesame seeds or Brazil nuts

CARBOHYDRATES

Essential for: fueling the body. Complex carbohydrates also contain fiber which supports the digestive system, helping eliminate wastes and toxins from the body.

Ideal percentage of diet: 65 percent
50 percent of daily intake: from fruits and vegetables: beans and peas, cabbage, cauliflower and broccoli, dark green leafy vegetables, fruits, pumpkin and squashes, root vegetables, seaweeds, sweet peppers
15 percent of daily intake: from grains: amaranth, brown rice, bulgar wheat, corn, millet, quinoa, rye, wheat, wholegrain breads and pastas

FATS

Essential for: energy. They also carry flavors and fat-soluble vitamins, make us feel full after meals and provide insulation, protecting delicate organs. Essential fats are needed for the nervous system, hormones, skin and brain function. They are especially important during pregnancy and breastfeeding for both mother and baby.

Ideal percentage of diet: 15 percent
Saturated fats: such as palm and coconut oil
Monounsaturated fats: such as olive oil and rapeseed oil
Polyunsaturated fats: omega-3 essential fats including soybeans, walnuts, rapeseed oil, hemp oil, flax oil; omega-6 essential fats including sunflower oil and sesame oil

NUTRIENTS AND THEIR SOURCES

Eat a varied diet and ensure that you incorporate all the nutrients listed below for a chance of living an extra ten healthy years compared with the average omnivore.

VITAMINS

KEY
RDA: Recommended Dietry Allowances as established by the US Department of Agriculture and The National Acadamies' Institute of Medicine for adults (19–50 years). The first figure is for women, second for men
AI: Adequate Intake as established by the USDA and IOM. AIs are set in the absence of sufficient data for RDAs
SONA: Suggested Optimal Nutritional Amount as set by University of Alabama, USA. Nutrient levels associated with highest health rating
mg/d : milligrams per day
mcg/d: micrograms per day

VITAMIN A (BETA-CAROTENE)
Essential for: growth, skin, vision, immunity, heart health
Adult RDA: 700–900mcg/d
Adult SONA: 2000mcg/d
Good sources: apricots (dried), carrots, chard, mangoes, melons (yellow), peppers (red and yellow), pumpkin, spinach, squash, strawberries, sweet potatoes, tomatoes, watercress

• VITAMIN B1 (THIAMIN)
Essential for: energy production (from carbohydrates), brain function, digestion
Adult RDA: 1.1–1.2mg/d
Adult SONA: 3.5-9.2mg/d
Good sources: beans and legumes, blackstrap molasses, brown rice, chickpeas, peanuts, soy products, sunflower seeds, wheatgerm, whole grains, yeast extract

• VITAMIN B2 (RIBOFLAVIN)
Essential for: energy production (fats and proteins); skin and internal membranes; nails and hair
Adult RDA: 1.1–1.3mg/d
Adult SONA: 1.8–2.5mg/d
Good sources: almonds, bamboo shoots, bean sprouts, broccoli, cabbage, green leafy vegetables, mushrooms, pumpkin, soy products, tomatoes, watercress, wheat germ, yeast extract

• VITAMIN B3 (NIACIN)
Essential for: brain and nerve function, skin, energy production, digestion
Adult RDA: 14–16mg/d
Adult SONA: 25–30mg/d
Good sources: asparagus, beets, cabbage, cauliflower, fruit (dried), millet, mushrooms, nuts, quinoa, squash, sunflower seeds, tomatoes, wholegrain cereals, yeast extract, zucchini

• VITAMIN B5 (PANTOTHENIC ACID)
Essential for: energy production, brain and nerve function, skin and hair, helps produce anti-stress hormones
Adult AI: 5mg/d

Adult SONA: 25mg/d
Good sources: alfalfa sprouts, avocados, broccoli, cabbage, celery, corn, lentils, mushrooms, peanuts, peas, tomatoes, soybeans, squash, strawberries, sunflower seeds, tomatoes, sunflower seeds, watercress, whole wheat

• VITAMIN B6 (PYRIDOXINE)
Essential for: protein conversion, growth, nervous and immune systems, heart health (via homocysteine regulation), brain function, hormone production, sex hormone balance
Adult RDA: 1.3mg/d
Adult SONA: 10–25mg/d
Good sources: avocados, bananas, broccoli, brown rice, Brussels sprouts, cabbage, carrots, cauliflower, red kidney beans, lentils, peppers (green, red and yellow), squash, soybeans, sunflower seeds, walnuts, watercress, wheat-germ, whole grains

• VITAMIN B9 (FOLATE, FOLIC ACID)
Essential for: blood cells, prevention of birth defects, protection against anemia
Adult RDA: 400 mcg/d
Adult SONA: 400–1000mcg/d
Good sources: asparagus, avocados, Brussels sprouts, bulgur wheat, kidney beans, root vegetables, soybeans, spinach, wheatgerm, whole grains

- **VITAMIN B12 (COBALAMIN)**
Essential for: energy production, nervous system, prevention of pernicious anemia, blood-cell formation, heart health (via homocysteine regulation), use of protein
Adult RDA: 2.4mcg/d
Adult SONA: 2–3mcg/d
Good sources: Take a reputable B12 supplement. Small amounts can also be found in breakfast cereals, non-hydrogenated margarines, sausage mixes, fortified soy milks, textured soy protein, yeast extract

- **BIOTIN**
Essential for: helping the body use essential fats to aid healthy skin, hair and nerves
Adult AI: 30mcg/d
Adult SONA: 50–200 mg/d
Good sources: almonds, brown rice, cabbage, cauliflower, legumes, lettuce, peas, sweet corn, tomatoes, whole grains

- **VITAMIN C (ASCORBIC ACID)**
Essential for: immunity, wound-healing, antioxidant properties, protection against heart disease and cancers, aiding iron absorption
Adult RDA: 75–90mg/d
Adult SONA: 400–1000mg/d
Good sources: alfalfa sprouts, berries, broccoli, cabbage, citrus fruits, cauliflower, currants, green vegetables, guavas, kale, kiwi fruit, lettuce, mangoes, parsley, peas, peppers (green, red and yellow), pineapple, potatoes, tomatoes

- **VITAMIN D**
Essential for: healthy bones, protection against osteoporosis
Adult RDA: 5–10mcg/d
Adult SONA: 10–20mcg/d
Good sources: fortified foods such as breakfast cereals, margarines, soy milk. Sunlight on the skin enables the body to manufacture its own vitamin D. Healthy adult vegans should be able to produce sufficient vitamin D if time is spent outdoors in the spring, summer and fall

- **VITAMIN E**
Essential for: antioxidant properties, heart and blood vessel protection, skin immunity, cancer-fighting
Adult AI: above 15mg/d
Adult SONA: 100–1000 mg/d
Good sources: avocado, blackstrap molasses, Brazil nuts, broccoli, cashew nuts, green leafy vegetables, olive oil, peanuts, safflower oil, spinach, sunflower oil, sunflower seeds, sweet potatoes, walnuts, watercress, wheatgerm

- **VITAMIN K**
Essential for: blood clotting, energy storage, liver function
Adult AI: 90–120mcg/kg/d
Adult SONA: 55–80 mcg/d
Good sources: alfalfa, blackstrap molasses, broccoli, cabbage, cauliflower, green leafy vegetables, kelp, lettuce, soybeans, spinach, strawberries, whole grains

MINERALS

- **CALCIUM**
Essential for: bone formation, prevention of osteoporosis, function of the heart, muscles and nerves
Adult AI: 1,000mg/d
Adult SONA: 800–1200mg/d
Good sources: almonds, apples, blackstrap molasses, Brazil nuts, broccoli, chickpeas, seaweed (dried), figs, fortified soy milk, green leafy vegetables, okra, parsley, quinoa, rutabaga, soybeans, tofu, watercress.

- **CHROMIUM**
Essential for: enabling the body to use glucose and maintain blood sugar levels and for gene expression
Adult AI: above 25–35mcg/d
Adult SONA: 100 mcg/d
Good sources: beans, brewer's yeast, nuts, whole grains

- **COPPER**
Essential for: respiration, nervous system, antioxidant properties, protein metabolism, bone formation
Adult RDA: 900mg/d
Adult SONA: not set
Good sources: almonds, avocados, blackstrap molasses, cauliflower, legumes (dried, especially soybeans), green leafy vegetables, nuts, whole grains

- **IODINE**
Essential for: normal functioning of the thyroid gland, which controls metabolism
Adult RDA: 150mcg/d
Adult SONA: not set
Good sources: green leafy vegetables, iodized salt, pears, seaweed, watercress, wild rice.

- **IRON**
Essential for: red blood cells, preventing anemia
Adult RDA: 18–8mg/d
Adult SONA: 15mg/d
Good sources: apricots (dried), beans, blackstrap molasses, cabbage, dark green leafy vegetables, dates, legumes, millet, nuts, parsley, plums (dried), pulses, pumpkin seeds, quinoa, raisins, seaweed (dried), sesame seeds, spinach, tofu, wheatgerm, wholegrain bread

- **MAGNESIUM**
Essential for: energy production, growth and repair, sleep, muscle relaxation
Adult RDA: 320–420mg/d
Adult SONA: 375–500mg/d
Good sources: almonds, bananas, blackstrap molasses, Brazil nuts, broccoli, brown rice, cashew nuts, dark green leafy vegetables, millet, peas, pine nuts, plums (dried), quinoa, sesame seeds, soybeans, sunflower seeds, wheatgerm, whole grains

- **MANGANESE**
Essential for: nervous system, sex hormone production, blood sugar regulation, skeletal development

Adult AI: 1.8–2.3mg/d
Adult SONA: 5mg/d
Good sources: green leafy vegetables, legumes, nuts, pineapple, most seeds, tea, whole grains

- **PHOSPHORUS**
Essential for: bones, teeth, metabolizing carbohydrates, heart contraction, kidney function
Adult RDA: 700mg/d
Adult SONA: not set
Good sources: broccoli, legumes, nuts, quinoa, whole grains

- **POTASSIUM**
Essential for: normal cell function, nerves, blood pressure control
Adult RDI: 3500mg/d
Adult SONA: 2000mg/d
Good sources: bananas, blackstrap molasses, chard, fruit (dried, especially apricots), fruit (fresh and juice), millet, nuts, quinoa, raw vegetables, seaweed, soybeans, spinach, sunflower seeds, tomatoes, wholegrain bread, yams

- **SELENIUM**
Essential for: antioxidant properties, protecting against heart disease and certain cancers, thyroid function
Adult RDA: 55mcg/d
Adult SONA: 100mcg/d
Good sources: acorn squash, avocados, Brazil nuts, lentils, mushrooms (fresh or dried), potatoes, sesame and sunflower seeds, walnuts, whole grains
Note: Selenium is dependent on soil levels, so eating organic foods can help

- **SODIUM**
Essential for: nerve transmission, maintaining body fluid levels
Adult RDA: 1600 mg/d
Adult SONA: 2400 mg/d
Intake: Generally too high. Recommended daily maximum for women is 5g and for men 7g.
Good sources: present in most foods

- **ZINC**
Essential for: growth, hormone function, male fertility, liver function, immunity, taste, protein digestion
Adult RDA: 8–11mg/d
Adult SONA: 15–20mg/d
Good sources: almonds, brown rice, seaweed, lentils, oats, pine nuts, pumpkin, sesame and sunflower seeds, wheatgerm, whole grains, wholegrain bread

NOTES
RDAs are based on minimum levels that prevent deficiency diseases but are not necessarily enough for optimum nutrition. SONAs also have been included to provide this information, where they have been set.

Remember that more is not always better: too much of any nutrient, especially fat-soluble nutrients such as vitamins A, D, E and K can also be damaging.

useful ingredients

The ingredients below are just some of the items that you might find useful to look for when shopping.

Acidophilus The "live" ingredient in yogurt, acidophilus is the friendly bacteria that ensures your digestive system is working smoothly. It's the arch-enemy of *Candida albicans*, the yeast that can cause upset stomachs if it grows unchecked.

Ackee This tropical fruit comes from an evergreen West African tree and is popular in the West Indies, particularly Jamaica. Because the unripe fruit and the parts surrounding it are poisonous, it's probably best to buy it in cans. Similar in flavor and texture to boiled egg yolk, ackee can be used in many dishes, including Thai curries, rice dishes and quiche, or just on toast with a little nutmeg. The Jamaicans add it to a tomato stew.

Agave syrup Sap from the cactus used to make tequila; a good alternative to honey and not usually quite as expensive as maple syrup.

Amaranth and **Quinoa** (pronounced "keen-wah") Both are pseudo-cereals because the seeds are technically fruits. These Peruvian grains are complete proteins, gluten-free and high in the amino acid lysine. They can be prepared and eaten in the same way as rice, bulgur wheat or couscous.

Avocado oil Deliciously rich and creamy, and excellent for cooking because it has a smoking point higher than most other vegetable oils.

Blackstrap molasses A thick brown residue obtained from sugar cane at the very end of the refining process. Containing iron and vitamin K, it can be used in baking instead of sugar, and combined with hot soy milk to make a delicious bedtime drink.

Bread Best buys are wholegrain and organic.

Calaloo West Indian spinach, often only available in cans. Prepare and use in the same way as spinach or kale.

Cassava Also known as manioc, this thick-skinned root vegetable originally came from Brazil but is now a staple foodstuff in South America and Africa. It may be ground into flour or peeled, chopped and cooked like potatoes. The flavor is similar to that of chestnuts, for which it may be substituted.

Cheese alternatives The characteristic flavors of cheese are sweetness (from lactose), richness (from saturated fat) and salt. Yeast flakes, vegan bouillon powder (Swiss) and vegan vegetable soup mixes with a high yeast content can add a cheesy flavor to sauces and cream made with plant milks. Dark yeast extract can do the same. Many varieties of vegan cheese are now available in supermarkets, but because they are low in sugar, fat and salt, many lack taste. There are a few that hit the spot, especially the new vegan cream cheeses, which you can roll in peppercorns, herbs or paprika to make them even more exciting.

Chlorella This comes in supplement or powder form and is high in phyto (plant) nutrients and B vitamins. It's basically pond-water algae, but you can easily disguise the taste by using the powder in a smoothie.

Chocolate Read the label to ensure the product contains cocoa butter rather than butterfat, and buy the best you can afford.

Cooking oils Use monounsaturates rather than polyunsaturates for cooking. Avocado oil and olive oil are both suitable. You should avoid hydrogenated fats, which contain trans-fatty acids, and keep saturated fats, such as coconut oil and palm oil, to a minimum.

Egg alternatives Among the things that will bind, emulsify or sometimes even taste a bit like eggs are ackee, agar agar, arrowroot, bananas, cornstarch, rice and powdered plant cellulose, soy flour, tofu and xanthum gum. Rice milk and self-rising flour make lovely pancakes, for instance. You can also buy various manufactured egg substitutes.

Fish alternatives Try smoked tofu, or check out your local healthfood store to find mercury-free, plant-based alternatives to fish. (They are also safe for pregnant women.)

Frozen vegetables Keep a selection in the freezer – they retain their nutrients (unlike fresh vegetables more than a few days old).

Gungo peas A popular pulse in Jamaica, with a taste and texture somewhere between a chickpea and a black-eyed pea. Any bean would do as an alternative.

Hemp seeds The size of grape seeds, hemp seeds are very nutritious, with balanced levels of essential omega-3 and 6 oils. They are best eaten raw. Hempseed oil has a nutty flavor and is delicious on salads.

Linseeds Also known as flaxseeds, these tiny seeds are rich in omega-3. Add to cereal, bread and all sorts of dishes.

Meat alternatives Tofu, tempeh and textured vegetable protein are perhaps the most common substitutes for meat, but chestnuts, mushrooms and various combinations of nuts and grains are full of protein and also make good alternatives. Stores now sell a huge variety of meat-free products, from vegan hotdogs to vegan giblet gravy.

Milk alternatives The variety is astonishing, including almond, barley, coconut, oat, pea, quinoa, rice and soy. Try rice milk on cereal, soy milk in sauces, coconut milk in ice cream, oat milk in custard, and any for smoothies.

Mustard A useful ingredient in sauces and dressings. Be sure that your Dijon mustard doesn't contain honey.

Pasta Like bread, buy wholegrain and organic varieties. Apart from the ubiquitous wheat, it is now possible to buy pasta made from almost any grain you can name, including buckwheat, corn and quinoa. Read the label to check eggs aren't among the ingredients.

Pectin The ingredient in certain fruits that helps jam to set. It has good detoxifying properties, and pure fruit pectin can sometimes be used as a gelatine substitute.

Rice Brown basmati rice is the best choice, as it is both nutritious and delicious. As with bread, buy wholegrain and organic varieties.

Salad oils Take advantage of all those delicious and nutritious polyunsaturated oils that should be consumed fresh and cold, such as pumpkin, hempseed and walnut.

Seaweed Japanese seaweeds are the best known and can be bought in mixed packs. Arame looks like thick, curly hair, while nori is available as flakes (good for sprinkling on soups or salads, like a herb) or flattened into sheets for making sushi. The Irish, Scots and Welsh maintain that their seaweeds are purer than Japanese varieties. These seaweeds have unique flavors and nutrients, and are a good source of iodine. Try Irish purple dulse (from healthfood stores or by mail order). Snip it into small pieces and add to stews and rice dishes.

Soy lecithin A natural emulsifier that helps the digestion of essential fats. It also contains choline, which helps to control liver and brain function and cholesterol levels. The granules may be sprinkled into ice cream, smoothies or cereals. Avoid egg lecithin.

Yeast extract A good ingredient for adding a "meaty" flavor to stews and gravies. Mixed with sweetened soy milk, it can also become quite cheesy in flavor.

Yeast flakes Nutritional yeast has a faintly cheesy flavor and is high in B vitamins. The dried flakes can be added to soups, salads or yogurt, or stirred into a basic white sauce to give it a cheesy flavor. Avoid yeast flakes if you have a digestive disorder arising from candida.

gungo peas

amaranth

calaloo

cassava

ackee

soy lecithin

chlorella

blackstrap molasses

yeast flakes

basic recipes

vegetable stock

Making your own stock allows you to use seasonal vegetables to vary the flavor.

preparation: 5–10 minutes
cooking: about 35 minutes
makes: 3½ cups

1 lb mixed vegetables, excluding potatoes, parsnips, or other starchy root vegetables, chopped
1 garlic clove
6 peppercorns
1 bouquet garni
4 cups water

1 Place all the ingredients in a large saucepan. Bring to a boil and simmer gently for 30 minutes, skimming when necessary.

2 Strain the stock, cool, then refrigerate it. It will keep for up to a week in the refrigerator, or up to 3 months in the freezer.

vegan cream cheese

Resembling ricotta, this cheese is especially good on toast with homemade jam. Alternatively, it can be eaten as a savory – rolled into balls and dipped in herbs, cracked black peppercorns or seaweed flakes.

preparation: 5 minutes
serves: 4

6 oz tofu
¼ cup coconut oil, melted
1 tablespoon rapeseed oil
1 tablespoon lime juice
1 tablespoon agave syrup
2 teaspoons salt

1 Place all the ingredients in a food processor or blender and combine well.

2 Transfer the mixture to a glass jar, store in the refrigerator and use as required. It will keep for up to 1 week.

vegan yogurt

Endlessly versatile, this yogurt can even be frozen.

preparation: 10 minutes, plus cooling and setting
cooking: 5 minutes
serves: 4

2 cups sweetened soy milk
2 tablespoons live vegan yogurt (unpasteurized) or 4 vegan acidophilus tablets

1 Sterilize the soy milk by heating it to just below boiling point.

2 Rinse a vacuum flask or large glass jar with boiling water to sterilize it.

3 Once the milk has cooled to lukewarm, pour it into your receptacle, stir in the live yogurt and put the lid on.

4 Place the container near a constant source of low heat, such as on top of the refrigerator. Alternatively, wrap it in a towel or newspaper and put it on a hot-water bottle. The yogurt should set within 12 hours. (If the temperature drops too low, it will stop the process or take longer; if the temperature is too high, the bacteria will be killed.)

5 Once set, refrigerate and use within 4–5 days. Keep 2 tablespoons of the yogurt to start off your next batch.

salad dressing

The great thing about this salad dressing, apart from its delicious taste, is that it contains a useful amount of the essential fats necessary for good health.

preparation: 5 minutes
serves: 4

¼ cup pumpkin seed oil or hempseed oil
1 tablespoon flax oil
1 tablespoon balsamic vinegar
2 teaspoons Dijon mustard
salt and pepper

1 Mix all the ingredients together and use as required. The dressing will keep for 1 week in the refrigerator.

soyannaise

Of course there's a vegan alternative to mayonnaise – and it tastes just as good as the real thing.

preparation: 5–10 minutes
cooking: 2 minutes
serves: 4

½ cup sweetened soy milk
pinch of salt
scant ½ cup sunflower oil
2½ teaspoons white wine vinegar
1 garlic clove, crushed (optional)
1 tablespoon Dijon mustard
2 tablespoons flax oil

1 Put the soy milk and salt in a saucepan and heat until hot, but not boiling.

2 While whisking the milk with an electric mixer or handheld blender, add the oil and vinegar.

3 Still whisking, add the crushed garlic, if using, mustard and flax oil. Refrigerate and use as required. It will keep for up to 1 week.

pizza base

Add any toppings you like to this simple homemade pizza base.

preparation: 10 minutes
cooking: 5 minutes
makes: 1 12-inch pizza base

1 tablespoon olive oil, plus extra for greasing
½ cup self-rising wholegrain flour
½ teaspoon chopped marjoram
2 scant tablespoons rice milk
1 teaspoon wine vinegar
¼ cup vegan yogurt (see page 14)
salt and pepper

1 Oil a baking sheet and preheat the oven to 350°F. Meanwhile, combine the base ingredients and knead for 10 minutes until smooth and shiny. Roll out to a 12-inch circle, place on the prepared baking sheet and bake for 5 minutes.

2 Remove the pizza base from the oven and brush with oil to make it liquid resistant. Continue with the recipe for the topping.

paprika yogurt dressing

Smoked paprika adds real depth of flavor to this dressing. Try it drizzled over an avocado or mixed-leaf salad

preparation: 5 minutes
serves: 6

8 oz soy yogurt
2 tablespoons pumpkin seed oil or hemp oil
2 tablespoons vegan tomato sauce
1 tablespoon flax oil
1 tablespoon balsamic vinegar
1 teaspoon smoked paprika
1 teaspoon finely grated lime rind
salt and pepper

1 Mix all the ingredients together and use immediately.

maple syrup dressing

Being sweet, this dressing is particularly good with the peppery taste of arugula, watercress and baby spinach leaves.

preparation: 4 minutes
serves: 6

2 tablespoons maple syrup
2 tablespoons cider vinegar
2 tablespoons sunflower oil
1 tablespoon soy sauce

1 Mix all the ingredients together and use as required. The dressing will keep for up to 1 week in the refrigerator.

red onion marmalade

Pâtés, vegan cheeses, cold pies, cold nut roast, falafel and hot sausages are all enhanced by a spoonful of this onion marmalade. It is also very good in sandwiches.

preparation: 10–15 minutes
cooking: 50–60 minutes
makes: 2 lb

2 unwaxed oranges, seeded and finely chopped
1 cup chopped red onion
1 cup vegetable stock (see page 14)
1 cup dark brown sugar
4 teaspoons arrowroot
½ cup apple pectin

1 Place the oranges, onion and vegetable stock in a medium saucepan, bring to a boil and simmer for 30–40 minutes, until the orange rind is tender.

2 Pour in the sugar and boil rapidly for 3–4 minutes, stirring occasionally. Add the arrowroot, stirring continuously as the liquid thickens. Remove the pan from the heat and stir in the pectin.

3 Allow the marmalade to cool a little, then pour into sterilized glass jars. When cold, cover and store until needed.

quick food fixes

Make time to eat and enjoy breakfast, and you will have a head start on the day in terms of nutrition and energy.

Ideally, think about breakfast the night before. Soak some oat flakes in apple juice for porridge, or make sure you have suitable things in the refrigerator or freezer, such as soy milk, sliced wholegrain bread or individual portions of frozen fruit. Try one, or a combination, of the following:

- Cereal bar and fruit juice.
- Mixture of nuts, seeds and fresh or dried fruit.
- vegan yogurt (see page 14) with nuts and seeds.
- Warmed wholegrain pita bread spread with yeast extract or soyannaise (see page 15) and filled with two vegan sausages or slices of vegan bacon.
- Oatcakes or rice cakes spread with pâté or vegan cream cheese (see page 14) plus fruit.
- Beans on toast.
- Nut butter and yeast extract on toast plus a banana.
- Raw carrot, piece of fruit cake and a glass of fortified plant milk.
- Toasted bagel with mashed tofu and yeast extract.

What do you do for lunch or a snack when you haven't had time to prepare your own? There are lots of vegan options available if you know where to look. Try some of the following:

- Nuts and seeds or Bombay mix.
- Fruits and vegetables, bought ready-prepared, are now available from many different stores.
- Vegan pies, sausages, ice creams and a variety of other treats can be found in most healthfood stores.
- Samosas, bhajis, pakoras or spring rolls are usually vegan and can be bought from Asian grocery stores.
- Hummus (chickpea dip) is delicious with crudités, olives and pita bread. Roll salad leaves and hummus in a tortilla wrap (minus milk powder).
- Pizza can be bought from a store or restaurant that allows you to create your own: just leave out the cheese and add lots of nutritious vegetables.

- Salsas with corn tortillas (minus milk powder) make a great lunch.
- Vegan pâté goes well with biscuits, oatcakes or breadsticks, with gherkins, pickles or mustard.
- Vegan sushi, available from upscale lunch bars.
- Spanish tapas and Greek meze bars offer numerous small dishes that are suitable for vegans.
- Baked potatoes, topped with anything you like.
- Fresh soups, from sandwich bars or supermarkets, are often OK for vegans. Just check that they don't contain any butter or cream.

TOP TEN SANDWICH IDEAS

The sandwich industry is big business, but far too few offerings are suitable for vegans. To redress the balance, here are ten ideas for making lunchtime tastier and more nutritious. Use any kind of bread that tickles your fancy, including tortillas and rice pancakes.

- Med Veg: roasted Mediterranean vegetables and olive hummus on sun-dried tomato bread.
- Gentleman's BLT: vegan "bacon steak" or smoked tofu, lettuce and tomato on thick bread.
- Phillymangerer: vegan cream cheese (see page 14), red peppers, garlic, chopped snow peas and celery.
- Scrambled Meg: breakfast scramble (see page 33) with nutmeg and watercress.
- Peanut Buttie: peanut butter with yeast extract, vegan coleslaw, bean sprouts and lettuce.
- Sushi Poochi: marinated and baked smoked tofu with sweet corn, nori seaweed flakes, pickled ginger, lettuce, lemon and capers in rice pancake wraps.
- Fungi Filler: wild mushroom, tarragon and lentil pâté with gherkins, red onion, watercress and alfalfa.
- Falafel-me-gently: chopped falafels, baba ghanoush (see page 59), sauerkraut, watercress, green onion, cucumber and parsley in a wholegrain roll.
- Dolly Pocket: vegan tuna or smoked tofu, capers, nori flakes, vegan tomato pesto, green onions, salad and soyannaise (see page 15) in a wholegrain pita.
- Bloody Mary: cherry tomatoes, sun-dried tomato paste, tahini, red kidney beans, red onion, gherkins. Jalapeño chile and black pepper in a corn tortilla.

breakfasts

preparation: 30–40 minutes, plus chilling and rising
cooking: 10–15 minutes
makes: 6

- 1½ teaspoons active dried yeast
- 1 teaspoon soft brown sugar
- ½ cup sweetened soy milk, warmed
- 2¼ cups all-purpose flour
- 1 teaspoon salt
- ¼ cup coconut oil, melted
- 3½ oz bar of dairy-free chocolate (optional)
- 1 tablespoon soyannaise (see page 15), to glaze

croissants

1 Mix the yeast with the sugar and the warm soy milk in a small bowl.

2 Place the flour and salt in a large bowl and mix in half the coconut oil. Make a well in the center, pour in the yeast mixture and gradually work it in with a fork to make a dough.

3 Flour a work surface and knead the dough for about 10 minutes until smooth. Roll out and spread with the remaining coconut oil. Cut the dough in half, put one half on top of the other, then roll up tightly. Wrap it in a plastic bag and put it in the refrigerator for 30 minutes.

4 When you're ready to make the croissants, divide the chilled dough into 3 pieces and roll each one into a square. Place the squares on separate pieces of wax paper, roll them up and chill until needed.

5 To make plain croissants, cut the squares in half diagonally, then roll them up loosely from the longest edge toward the point. Bring the 2 ends around to touch each other, making a crescent shape.

6 To make chocolate croissants, place 2 squares of chocolate in the triangles and roll them up as described in step 5.

7 Preheat the oven to 350°F. Leave the croissants to rise for 30 minutes. Glaze the tops of the croissants with soyannaise and bake for 10–15 minutes, depending how brown you like them.

essential seed snack bars

Essential seed mix
- 2 tablespoons pumpkin seeds
- 2 tablespoons sunflower seeds
- 2 tablespoons sesame seeds
- ⅛ cup hemp seeds
- ⅛ cup linseeds

Snack bars
- 1 cup rolled oats
- ¼ cup dried dates, finely chopped
- ¼ cup dried apricots, finely chopped
- 2 tablespoons coconut, finely grated
- 2 teaspoons carob powder
- 1 tablespoon brown rice flour
- 1 tablespoon blackstrap molasses
- 1 tablespoon agave or maple syrup
- 2 tablespoons lime juice

This recipe is based on essential seed mix (left), which provides an excellent way of upping your intake of protein and essential fatty acids. It can be used in many different ways – on cereal, in sandwiches, on salads, in soups or even in ice cream – but should not be used in cooking. Here it is used to make delicious snack bars.

1 To make the essential seed mix, grind the pumpkin, sunflower and sesame seeds in a food processor. Take care not to over-grind, or the sesame will turn to "putty." Grind the hemp seeds and linseeds in an herb mill or coffee grinder. Combine the 2 mixtures and transfer to a dark glass jar with a tight-fitting lid. It can be stored in the refrigerator for up to 4 days.

2 Mix all the dry ingredients for the bars in a bowl. Add ¼ cup of essential seed mix, the molasses, agave syrup and lime juice and and stir thoroughly.

3 Divide the mixture into 4, then roll into short sausage shapes and pat to flatten into bars.

4 Wrap the snack bars tightly in wax paper and place in an airtight container. They can be stored in the refrigerator for up to 4 days.

high-protein smoothie

preparation: 5 minutes
serves: 1

Both Canada and the US claim to have created smoothies back in the 1970s, but the worldwide craze for them didn't really take off until the 1990s. Now smoothie bars are everywhere, but it's easy (and cheaper) to make your own at home.

1 Place all the ingredients in a blender and mix until smooth.

2 Mix in the chlorella algae and yogurt, if using, and serve.

- 1 banana
- ½ mango
- 1 tablespoon essential seed mix (see page 20)
- 1 tablespoon chopped mixed dried fruit, e.g., apricots, figs, raisins, peaches, blueberries, bananas, papaya, or 2 tablespoons fresh berries
- 1 cup soy, rice or oat milk, chilled
- 1 Brazil nut, chopped
- 1 walnut, chopped
- 1 tablespoon chlorella algae (optional)
- 1 tablespoon vegan yogurt (optional, see page 14)

- 2 cups oat breakfast flakes
- ½ cup pumpkin seeds
- ½ cup sunflower seeds
- 1 cup mixed dried fruit, e.g., apricots, figs, raisins, blueberries, pineapple, bananas, peaches, papaya, chopped
- 6 Brazil nuts, chopped
- 6 walnuts, chopped

high-protein muesli

It has been claimed that muesli was pioneered in the 1890s by Max Bircher-Benner, a Swiss doctor who called cereals, fruits and vegetables "food of the sunlight." As these were then considered food for poor people, his peers gave him quite a hard time. For maximum nutrition, add a spoonful of essential seed mix (see page 20) and soy, pea, almond or quinoa milk to each serving.

1 Mix all the ingredients together and store in an airtight container in a cool, dark place. Serve with slices of fruit or berries and a spoonful of vegan yogurt (see page 14).

preparation: 3 minutes
cooking: 15 minutes
serves: 1

- 1 cup rolled oats
- 1 tablespoon rapeseed oil
- 1 tablespoon blackstrap molasses
- 1 tablespoon soy milk

toasted granola

This delicious cereal will keep for a few weeks if stored in an airtight container. Serve with soy milk or vegan yogurt (see page 14).

1 Preheat the oven to 350°F. Place all the ingredients in a bowl and stir well so that the oats form clusters.

2 Tip the mixture into a large, shallow tin and bake for 15 minutes.

3 Allow to cool, then store in an airtight container until needed.

porridge

preparation: 3 minutes
cooking: 12 minutes
serves: 4

Those on a gluten-free diet can use millet, rice or quinoa instead of oats in this recipe.

1 Place the oats, salt and milk in a large saucepan, bring to a boil, then simmer gently, stirring frequently with a wooden spoon, for about 10 minutes.

2 Stir in the sunflower oil and continue cooking for another 1–2 minutes.

3 Serve the porridge with small bowls of essential seed mix, chopped dried fruit, maple syrup and soy cream offered separately.

- 1⅓ cups rolled oats
- 1 teaspoon salt
- 2 cups rice milk or soy milk
- 1 tablespoon sunflower oil

To serve
- 3 tablespoons essential seed mix (see page 20)
- ¼ cup chopped mixed dried fruit
- ¼ cup maple syrup
- ¼ cup soy cream

- 2¼ cups self-rising wholegrain flour
- pinch of salt
- 2 cups rice milk or soy milk
- 1 tablespoon lime juice
- rapeseed oil, for frying

pancakes

This recipe makes fairly thin pancakes; if you prefer very thick ones, use more flour. Stir a handful of raisins into the batter if you like fruity pancakes, which are particularly delicious cold.

1 Mix the flour and salt with the milk and lime juice and beat together to make a smooth batter.

2 Heat a heavy nonstick frying pan until very hot, then pour in a dribble of rapeseed oil and swirl it around the pan.

3 Add just enough pancake mix to barely cover the bottom of the pan in a thin, even layer. Cook for about a minute, until the bottom has set and become lightly browned, then flip the pancake over and cook the other side.

4 Serve the pancakes hot, spread with vegan cream cheese (see page 14) and jam or maple syrup. If you prefer a savory breakfast, top the pancakes with the cream cheese plus yeast extract and gherkins.

preparation: 10 minutes
cooking: 5 minutes
serves: 2

grapefruit salad

- 1 pink grapefruit, halved horizontally
- 2 teaspoons soft brown sugar
- ½ teaspoon cinnamon
- ¼ cup coconut cream or vegan yogurt (see page 14)

To serve
- 2 strawberries
- 1 banana, halved
- 1 apple, cored and cut into 6 segments
- 1 orange, segmented
- 12 seedless grapes
- 1 small papaya, seeded, peeled and cut into segments
- 2 tablespoons berries
- 1 thick slice pineapple, cut into 6 segments

Thought to be a mutation of the West Indian pomelo fruit, grapefruit has long been a favorite at breakfast-time. The pink-fleshed variety is especially good.

1 Preheat the grill to medium, or preheat the oven to 350°F. Cut a sliver from the base of each grapefruit half so that they sit level. Cut around the edge of the flesh and between the segments.

2 Mix together the sugar and cinnamon, then rub into the grapefruit flesh. Place the grapefruit halves on a baking sheet and grill for 5 minutes, or heat in the oven for 10 minutes, until the sugar has caramelized.

3 Meanwhile, prepare the strawberries. Starting just below the top to keep the stalk end intact, make several thin cuts right through the berries down to the point. Gently fan out the fruit. Prepare the banana halves in a similar way. Cut wedges from the center of the apple segments to make "steps."

4 Stir any remaining sugar and cinnamon into the coconut cream, then divide between 2 ramekins.

5 Place each grapefruit half on a plate with a ramekin of coconut cream. Arrange the prepared fruit around the edge of the plate, placing a strawberry fan on top of the grapefruit.

creamy mushrooms on toast

preparation: 5 minutes
cooking: 10 minutes
serves: 2

Mushrooms contain B vitamins, calcium, magnesium and zinc, so are a great choice for a healthy breakfast.

1 Preheat the oven to 350°F. Place the bread on a baking sheet and bake for 5 minutes.

2 Meanwhile, heat the oil in a frying pan, add the lime juice and fry the onion and mushrooms until soft. Stir in the soy sauce, followed by the soy cream.

3 Cut the toast into triangles and arrange on plates in a star shape. Pour the mushroom mix on top, then garnish with a sprinkling of parsley and a slice of lime.

- 4 slices wholegrain bread
- 1 tablespoon avocado oil
- 1 tablespoon lime juice
- 1 small onion, chopped
- 8 mushrooms, sliced
- 1 tablespoon soy sauce
- 2 tablespoons soy cream or vegan yogurt or soyannaise (see page 14 or 15)

To garnish
- 2½ teaspoons chopped parsley
- 2 slices of lime

- 2½ teaspoons soy sauce
- 2 teaspoons avocado oil or olive oil
- 2 oz smoked tofu or vegan bacon or ham, finely chopped
- ½ cup sweetened soy milk
- ½ cup rapeseed oil
- 2½ teaspoons cider vinegar
- 1 tablespoon potato flour
- 1 teaspoon spicy brown mustard
- 1 tablespoon vegan tomato sauce
- 1 teaspoon vegan bouillon powder
- 4 slices wholegrain bread
- 1 teaspoon yeast extract
- black pepper

smoky tofu nuggets on toast

1 Preheat the oven to 350°F. Combine the soy sauce and avocado oil in a small bowl, then add the smoked tofu and mix well. Spoon the tofu mixture on to an oiled baking sheet and place in the oven for 10–15 minutes or until crispy.

2 Heat the soy milk to just below boiling point. Add the rapeseed oil and mix thoroughly with a hand-held whisk. Add the vinegar, whisking all the time.

3 Add the potato flour, mustard, tomato sauce and bouillon powder to the milk mixture, whisk again and bring back to a boil, stirring constantly.

4 Spread the slices of bread with yeast extract.

5 Mix the baked tofu with the milk mixture, then spread on the bread.

6 Place the bread on the baking sheet and bake in the oven for 10 minutes until golden and starting to bubble. Cut each slice into wedges and sprinkle with black pepper.

bubble and squeak

- 1 small onion, chopped
- 2 tablespoons self-rising wholegrain flour
- 2 tablespoons mashed or baked potatoes
- 2 tablespoons finely chopped red cabbage
- 1 tablespoon olive oil
- 1 tablespoon soy milk
- 1 teaspoon Dijon mustard
- salt and pepper
- 1 tablespoon coconut oil, for frying

Some of the best recipe ideas are based on leftovers, and this traditional British recipe is a fine example.

1 Mix all the ingredients together, except for the oil, and form into 4 burger shapes.

2 Heat the coconut oil in a nonstick frying pan, then fry the burgers on both sides over medium heat until golden brown.

3 Serve with hot baked beans and mushrooms or scrambled tofu.

breakfast scramble

preparation: 5 minutes
cooking: 15 minutes
serves: 2

Although there are egg substitutes available, most of them are binding agents rather than true egg alternatives. The tofu, cauliflower and sweet corn in this recipe all have whole egg–like properties.

1 Steam the cauliflower for about 10 minutes until soft.

2 Meanwhile, place the sweet corn and milk in a small saucepan, bring to the boil and simmer for about 5 minutes until soft. Blend the mixture or mash with a fork.

3 Add the oil, turmeric, crumbled tofu, cauliflower and salt and pepper, then simmer, stirring, until hot.

4 Toast the bread. Spread the soyannaise on the toast, then top with the steamed cauliflower and tofu mix.

5 To garnish, sprinkle with a pinch of nutmeg and add a sprig of parsley and some tomato wedges.

- 1 cup finely chopped cauliflower
- 3 tablespoons frozen sweet corn
- ¼ cup oat milk
- 2½ teaspoons avocado oil or rapeseed oil
- 1 teaspoon turmeric
- 4 oz tofu, crumbled
- 4 slices wholemeal bread
- 1 tablespoon soyannaise (see page 15)
- salt and pepper

To garnish
- pinch of nutmeg
- sprig of parsley
- tomato wedges

egg-free omelette

- 4 tablespoons olive oil
- 1 onion, chopped
- 6 mushrooms, sliced
- ½ red pepper, seeded and chopped
- ½ green pepper, seeded and chopped
- 2 oz tofu, crumbled
- 5 tablespoons soy milk
- 3 heaping tablespoons bread flour
- 1 tablespoon cider vinegar
- 1 tablespoon soy sauce
- 2 heaping teaspoons vegan bouillon powder
- 2 teaspoons herbes de Provence
- 1 teaspoon mustard
- ½ teaspoon baking powder
- 1 tablespoon soyannaise (see page 15)
- salt and pepper

Although this recipe uses no eggs at all, it's a real winner. For an interesting variation, try adding grated vegan cheese, vegan bacon bits or pumpkin seeds to the mix.

1 Heat 1 tablespoon of the oil in a large nonstick frying pan, then gently fry the onion, mushrooms, peppers and tofu over medium heat for about 5 minutes, stirring occasionally.

2 Place the milk, flour, vinegar, soy sauce, bouillon powder, herbes de Provence, mustard, baking powder, 2 tablespoons of the oil and salt and pepper in a large bowl and whisk with a fork.

3 Fold in the soyannaise, then pour the mixture on to the vegetables in the pan. Cook gently for 3–4 minutes with the pan covered so that the steam partly cooks the top.

4 Slide the omelette on to a plate, then oil the pan, place it upside down over the plate and flip over. Return the pan to the heat and brown the other side of the omelette. Serve hot with a mixed salad.

chapter two

light meals

preparation: 15 minutes
cooking: about 20 minutes
serves: 2

- 3 tablespoons vegan cream cheese (see page 14)
- 1 garlic clove, chopped
- 1 tablespoon chopped parsley
- 8 peppadew peppers, tops removed, seeded
- 1 cup plus 2 tablespoons bread flour
- ½ cup rice milk or soy milk
- 1 tablespoon vegan yogurt (see page 14)
- 1 teaspoon arrowroot
- 1 teaspoon vegan bouillon powder
- 1 teaspoon finely grated lime zest
- 1 tablespoon coconut oil
- sesame seeds, for sprinkling

crispy, stuffed peppadew peppers

Peppadew peppers are mild, sweet South African mini peppers. If you can't find them, any baby pepper or large chile can be used, although you should avoid using Scotch bonnet or habañero peppers, as they are potently fiery.

1 Grease a baking sheet. Preheat the oven to 350°F.

2 Place the cream cheese, garlic and parsley in a bowl and mix together thoroughly. Put a teaspoonful of the cream cheese mixture into each of the peppers.

3 Place the flour, milk, yogurt, arrowroot, bouillon powder and lime zest in a small bowl or jug and mix well to make a stiff batter.

4 Dip each stuffed pepper into the batter to coat the outside, then place on the prepared baking sheet.

5 Sprinkle the peppers with the oil and sesame seeds, then bake for about 7 minutes. Baste, then return to the oven for another 7–10 minutes, until crisp.

- **3 teaspoons olive oil**
- **¼ cup frozen sweet corn**
- **2 tablespoons self-rising wholegrain flour**
- **1 teaspoon vegan bouillon powder**
- **2 tablespoons soy milk**
- **1 teaspoon cider vinegar**
- **2½ teaspoons chopped chives**
- **black pepper**
- **sweet chile sauce, to serve**

corn fritters

For an interesting variation, try adding very finely chopped vegan bacon to the basic sweet corn mixture.

1 Preheat the oven to 350°F. Heat 1 teaspoonful of the oil in a frying pan and fry the sweet corn for a few minutes until it is hot.

2 Combine the flour, bouillon powder, milk, vinegar, chives and pepper in a bowl. Add the sweet corn to the flour mixture and stir thoroughly.

3 Heat the remaining oil in the frying pan, then add tablespoonfuls of the corn mixture, spacing them well apart. Fry on both sides until light golden brown.

4 Transfer the fritters to a baking tin and bake for 5–10 minutes until they rise a little. Serve with sweet chile sauce for dipping.

tomato bombs

- 4 large tomatoes
- 8 plump black olives, pitted and chopped
- 1 garlic clove, finely chopped
- ¼ cup vegan cream cheese (see page 14)
- 2 tablespoons olive oil
- 1 teaspoon finely chopped parsley
- 1 teaspoon finely chopped marjoram or oregano
- salt and pepper

To garnish
- essential seed mix (see page 20)
- smoked paprika

These are perfect for a summer lunch. As an alternative, you could stuff the tomatoes with seaweed, sticky rice and smoked tofu for a sushi-type dish.

1 Slice a very thin sliver off the bottom of each tomato so that they sit level on a plate. Cut off the tops and scoop out the seeds and juice into a small bowl. Discard the hard tomato cores.

2 Add the olives, garlic, cream cheese, olive oil, parsley, marjoram and salt and pepper to the bowl of tomato juice and mix well.

3 Stuff the tomatoes with the mixture, taking care not to split them.

4 Garnish the tomatoes with a little essential seed mix and a dusting of smoked paprika. Serve with a mixed salad and ciabatta bread.

papaya with guacamole

preparation: 15 minutes
cooking: 5 minutes
serves: 4

Papayas are believed to have originated in southern Mexico but are now grown in many parts of the tropics. Their nutritional attributes include useful levels of calcium, magnesium, potassium, vitamin C and beta-carotene.

1 Preheat the oven to 350°F.

2 Cut the avocado in half, remove the stone and scoop the flesh into a small bowl. Add the yogurt, lime juice, garlic and salt and mix to a smooth consistency using a handheld mixer or a blender.

3 Wash and dry the papayas, cut them in half, then scoop out the seeds. Cut a sliver off the bottom of each papaya half so that they sit level on individual serving plates.

4 Heat the pita breads in the oven for about 5 minutes, until warm.

5 Fill each papaya with guacamole and garnish with slices of lime and a sprinkle of smoked paprika. Cut the pita breads into triangles and arrange around the papaya halves.

- 1 large avocado
- 2 tablespoons vegan yogurt (see page 14) or soy milk
- juice of $\frac{1}{2}$ lime
- 1 garlic clove, crushed
- 2 pear-sized papayas
- salt
- 2 wholegrain pita breads

To garnish
- 1 lime, sliced
- $\frac{1}{2}$ teaspoon smoked paprika

- 2 large flat field mushrooms
- 2 tablespoons olive oil, plus
  extra for oiling
- 2 green onions, chopped
- ½ red pepper, seeded and
  chopped
- 1 small zucchini, chopped
- 4 olives, pitted and chopped
- 2 tablespoons rolled oats
- 1 tablespoon chopped basil
- 1 tablespoon soy sauce
- 1 tablespoon lime juice
- salt and pepper
- mixed greens, to serve

stuffed mushrooms

"Stuffed mushrooms" is not really a strictly accurate name for this dish, because the mushrooms are used as a platter or basket for the stuffing. It makes a great dish for a special occasion breakfast or a starter. As a variation, you can use chopped apricots instead of the red peppers and a tart apple instead of the zucchini.

1 Preheat the oven to 350°F. Wipe the mushrooms clean with a damp paper towel, then remove the stalks and chop them.

2 Heat the oil in a small saucepan and gently fry the chopped mushroom stalks, green onions, red pepper, zucchini, olives and oats until the oats are golden. Stir in the basil, soy sauce and lime juice.

3 Oil the mushroom caps and place them on a baking sheet. Spoon the oat mixture into the mushrooms, season with salt and pepper, and bake for 15–20 minutes, until the caps start to soften.

4 Serve the hot mushrooms immediately on a bed of mixed greens.

Pancakes
- **⅔ cup self-rising wholegrain flour**
- **2 teaspoons Atlantic seaweed flakes or your favorite herbs**
- **1 teaspoon smoked paprika**
- **½ teaspoon salt**
- **black pepper**
- **1½ cups rice milk**
- **avocado oil, for frying**
- **2 lime wedges, to garnish (optional)**

Filling
- **8 asparagus spears, trimmed**
- **1 cup soy milk**
- **2½ teaspoons cornstarch**
- **1 garlic clove, chopped**
- **2 tablespoons vegan port or sherry**
- **1 tablespoon olive oil**
- **2 teaspoons cider vinegar**
- **2 teaspoons Dijon mustard**
- **1 teaspoon vegan bouillon powder**

asparagus pancakes

1 Set the oven to low heat, about 275°F. Place all the dry pancake ingredients in a bowl and mix in the rice milk to make a lump-free batter. Cover and chill.

2 Meanwhile, make the filling. Place the asparagus spears in a vegetable steamer and cook for 10 minutes, until they have softened.

3 Pour the soy milk into a small saucepan, stir in the cornstarch and heat until the mixture starts to thicken. Add the remaining ingredients, stirring constantly.

4 To cook the pancakes, heat a frying pan until hot, then pour in a drizzle of avocado oil and swirl it around the pan. Whisk the chilled batter, then pour half into the pan, tilting it to spread it out evenly. When the bottom is set and speckled light brown, turn the pancake over and cook the other side. Place in the oven to keep warm, then make the second pancake.

5 To serve, divide the filling between the 2 pancakes, place 4 whole asparagus spears on top of each one, then fold them over and serve immediately on hot plates, garnished with a lime wedge, if using.

preparation: 10 minutes
cooking: 15–20 minutes
serves: 2

- 2 English muffins or 4 crumpets
- ¼ cup vegan tomato sauce
- ¼ cup soyannaise (see page 15)
- 1 teaspoon Dijon mustard
- 1 teaspoon yeast extract
- 1 mushroom, cut into 4 slices
- 4 olives
- salt and pepper

pizza muffins

Children love these pizza muffins as party food or just as a snack. Grown-ups might like to replace the English muffin with a thick round slice of fried eggplant.

1 Preheat the oven to 180°C (350°F), Gas Mark 4. Split the muffins in half. (If you are using crumpets, leave them whole.)

2 Spread some tomato sauce on each muffin half.

3 Mix together the soyannaise, mustard and yeast extract in a bowl, then place a spoonful on top of each muffin. Put a slice of mushroom and an olive on the top and bake for about 15–20 minutes, until the topping is golden and begins to bubble.

4 Season the muffins with salt and pepper and serve with a mixed green salad or vegan coleslaw.

savory cookie swirls

preparation: 15 minutes

cooking: 25 minutes

makes: 18

These savory swirls are very pretty; they make perfect party food and are good for picnics and packed lunches, and children enjoy them too. If you are cooking for people who don't like spicy food, use paprika instead of the chiles.

1 Grease a baking sheet. Preheat the oven to 350°F.

2 Place the flour, oil, bouillon powder and soy milk in a bowl, mix together to form a dough, then divide into 3 equal pieces. On a floured work surface, roll out the dough into rectangles measuring 6 x 4 inches.

3 Spread the seaweed tapenade and chopped mushrooms on one rectangle; the red pesto and chopped red peppers and chiles on another; and the cream cheese, green onions and herbs on the third.

4 Roll each sheet up from a short end and cut each roll into 6 pieces. Place the savory swirls on the prepared baking sheet, brush the tops with oil and bake for 25 minutes.

5 Serve the swirls hot with soup or cold with a selection of dips.

- 1½ cups self-rising wholegrain flour
- ½ cup rapeseed oil, plus extra for greasing
- 1 teaspoon vegan bouillon powder
- ½ cup soy milk
- 1 tablespoon seaweed tapenade (see page 64)
- 2 tablespoons chopped mushrooms
- 1 tablespoon red pesto sauce
- 2 tablespoons chopped red pepper and chiles
- 1 heaping tablespoon vegan cream cheese (see page 14)
- 1 tablespoon chopped green onions
- 1 tablespoon chopped mixed basil and parsley

- **1 small butternut squash**
- **2 beets**
- **1 potato**
- **½ cassava (see page 11)**
- **2 carrots**
- **2 red onions**
- **1 zucchini**
- **½ cup avocado oil**
- **1 tablespoon soy sauce**
- **4 whole garlic cloves**
- **2½ teaspoons rosemary leaves**
- **2½ teaspoons chopped fennel fronds**
- **salt and pepper**

roasted vegetables

1 Preheat the oven to 350°F. Scrub and trim all the vegetables, then cut them into finger-sized pieces.

2 Place the avocado oil and soy sauce in a large bowl and mix well. Dip in the vegetable pieces and garlic so that they are well coated.

3 Arrange the squash, beets, potato and cassava pieces on a baking tray and bake for 20 minutes.

4 Turn these vegetables over, then add the carrots, onions, zucchini and garlic. Sprinkle with the rosemary and fennel, season with salt and pepper, then return the tray to the oven for another 25–30 minutes.

5 Serve with a variety of dips, such as hummus, soyannaise (see page 15) or sweet chile sauce, and some warm bread.

preparation: **5** minutes
cooking: **7** minutes
serves: **2**

spicy avocado toast

- **1 tablespoon olive oil**
- **¼ cup roughly chopped avocado or canned ackee**
- **1 onion, finely chopped**
- **1 green chile, finely chopped (optional)**
- **2 pinches of nutmeg**
- **2 slices rye bread**
- **1 tablespoon plus 1 teaspoon hempseed oil or pumpkin seed oil**
- **salt and pepper**

To garnish
- **2½ teaspoons chopped parsley or seaweed flakes**
- **2 lime slices**

The avocado originated in central America and is now a major crop in many parts of the world. A source of vitamin E, it is becoming increasingly important as the source of the perfect healthy cooking oil because of its high level of monosaturated fats.

1 Heat the oil in a small saucepan, then add the avocado, onion, chile, if using, and nutmeg and season with salt and pepper. Fry gently until the onion is soft.

2 Lightly toast the rye bread.

3 Drizzle the hempseed oil onto the toast, then spoon the hot avocado mixture on top.

4 Arrange the toast on warm plates, sprinkle with parsley and garnish with the lime slices.

pea soufflettes

preparation: 10 minutes
cooking: 25 minutes
serves: 4

These little soufflés taste great hot or cold and make a satisfying lunch if served with some mixed greens and crusty bread. They're also ideal picnic fare.

1 Grease four 3¼-inch ramekins. Preheat the oven to 350°F.

2 Divide 2 oz of the peas among the 4 ramekins and top each one with a teaspoon of yogurt.

3 Place all the remaining ingredients, except for the vinegar, in a bowl, and mix thoroughly using a handheld mixer or a blender. Add the vinegar and mix again.

4 Pour the mixture into the ramekins and bake for about 25 minutes, until golden brown on top and a toothpick inserted in the middle comes out clean.

- 1 cup frozen peas
- 4 teaspoons vegan yogurt (see page 14)
- 1⅓ cups self-rising wholegrain flour
- 1 cup sweetened soy milk
- 1 tablespoon rapeseed oil
- 1 tablespoon chopped apple mint
- 2 teaspoons vegan bouillon powder
- 1 tablespoon cider vinegar

crispy duckless pancakes

preparation: 10 minutes
cooking: 20–25 minutes
serves: 4

- 2 tablespoons avocado oil
- 1 tablespoon soy sauce
- 1 tablespoon blackstrap molasses
- 6 mushrooms, sliced
- 1 onion, finely chopped
- 8 oz mock duck or tofu, crumbled
- 12 rice pancakes, fresh or dried
- 6 green onions, sliced into lengths
- 1 cucumber, sliced into short lengths
- 1 lime, quartered
- 6 tablespoons vegan oyster sauce
- 2 tablespoons sesame seeds

Mock duck is a meat substitute from the Far East. It is readily available in cans and may also be found frozen, in a duck shape, in Chinese supermarkets. If using dried rather than fresh rice pancakes, provide individual bowls of hot water so that people can soak their own pancakes for 30 seconds as they need them. Afterward the water can be used for rinsing sticky fingers.

1 Grease a baking sheet. Preheat the oven to 350°F.

2 Mix the oil, soy sauce and molasses in a bowl, then add the mushrooms, onion and mock duck and stir thoroughly to coat.

3 Place a thin layer of the mock duck mixture on the prepared baking sheet and bake for 20–25 minutes, until crispy.

4 Heat the rice pancakes according to the package instructions.

5 Place the mock duck, green onions, cucumber, lime, oyster sauce and sesame seeds in separate serving bowls.

6 At the table, spread a teaspoonful of oyster sauce on a warm pancake. Top with a spoonful of mock duck, a few sticks of cucumber, a spoonful of green onion, a sprinkling of sesame seeds and a squeeze of lime juice, then roll up and eat.

potato, sea vegetable and leek soup

- **2 potatoes, scrubbed and chopped**
- **2 cups vegetable stock (see page 14)**
- **2 leeks, finely chopped**
- **2 garlic cloves, chopped**
- **1 cup rice milk**
- **2 tablespoons olive oil**
- **2 tablespoons mixed Atlantic sea vegetable flakes or finely chopped dulse**
- **2 tablespoons cider vinegar**
- **2½ teaspoons miso paste**
- **2 teaspoons mustard powder**
- **salt and pepper**

To garnish
- **pumpkin seed oil**
- **essential seed mix (see page 20)**

The addition of sea vegetables to the old favorite potato and leek soup not only adds extra flavor and texture, it also enhances the nutritional value of the dish. Because they contain calcium, iron and potassium, sea vegetables are good for heart health and can help rid the body of toxins.

1 Place the potatoes and vegetable stock in a large saucepan, bring to a boil and simmer for 10 minutes.

2 Add all the remaining ingredients and simmer for another 10 minutes. Transfer to a food processor or blender and mix to a smooth consistency.

3 Serve the soup in warm bowls with a drizzle of pumpkin seed oil and a sprinkling of essential seed mix, and accompany by warm ciabatta bread.

broccoli and peanut soup

preparation: 10 minutes
cooking: 15–20 minutes
serves: 4

Broccoli really is a wonder food that has enjoyed great success in many studies investigating its protection against a range of diseases including heart disease and Alzheimer's. It has revered antioxidant properties and contains calcium, magnesium, phosphorus, vitamins B3, B5, C and beta-carotene and high levels of folic acid.

1 Place the broccoli, onion and oat milk in a large saucepan, bring to a boil and simmer for 10–15 minutes, until softened.

2 Transfer the mixture to a food processor or blender and mix to a smooth consistency. Add the oil, peanut butter and bouillon powder and season with salt and pepper, then blend again. With the processor or blender still running, add the cider vinegar.

3 Return the soup to the pan and reheat gently. Serve in warm bowls with hot, crusty bread and a sprinkling of essential seed mix.

- 10 oz purple-sprouting broccoli, chopped
- 1 onion, chopped
- 2 cups oat milk or soy milk
- 2 tablespoons olive oil
- 2 tablespoons peanut butter
- 1 tablespoon vegan bouillon powder
- 2 tablespoons cider vinegar
- salt and pepper
- essential seed mix (see page 20), to garnish

preparation: 10 minutes
cooking: 50 minutes
serves: 8

- 6 medium beets, peeled and chopped
- 2 red onions, chopped
- 1 garlic clove, chopped
- 4 cups vegetable stock (see page 14)
- ½ cup dried apricots, chopped
- 1 tablespoon lime juice
- 1 teaspoon cumin
- 1 teaspoon paprika
- 2 cups orange juice
- salt and pepper

To garnish
- soy cream
- 2 tablespoons pumpkin seed oil
- 2 tablespoons chopped coriander leaves

apricot, beet and cumin soup

The purée base of this soup is ideal for freezing in individual portions. For a quick and tasty lunch, simply defrost, dilute with orange juice and heat through.

1 Place the beets, onions, garlic, vegetable stock, apricots, lime juice, cumin and paprika in a large saucepan. Bring to a boil, then cover and simmer gently for 45 minutes.

2 Transfer the mixture to a food processor or blender and mix until smooth. (The soup can be frozen at this point.)

3 Add the orange juice, then season to taste with salt and pepper. Garnish the soup with a swirl of soy cream, a little pumpkin seed oil and a sprinkling of coriander leaves.

tomato and orange soup with garlic ciabatta

preparation: 10 minutes
cooking: 20–25 minutes
serves: 4

- 2 tablespoons avocado oil
- 2 garlic cloves, chopped
- 4 ready-to-bake ciabatta rolls
- 2 tablespoons olive oil
- 2 carrots, chopped
- 1 red onion, chopped
- 2 lbs tomatoes, chopped
- 1 red pepper, seeded and chopped
- 1 small red chile pepper, seeded and chopped
- 4 dried apricots, chopped
- 2 cups orange juice
- ¼ cup ginger wine
- 1 tablespoon paprika
- 1 tablespoon cider vinegar
- salt and pepper

To garnish
- soy cream
- 1 tablespoon chopped parsley

1 Preheat the oven to 350°F. Place the avocado oil, garlic and salt and pepper in a small bowl and mix well.

2 Slice the rolls in half and spread with the garlic oil mixture. Wrap in foil and bake for 15 minutes.

3 Meanwhile, heat the olive oil in a large saucepan and gently fry the carrots and onion until the onions are soft. Add the tomatoes, red pepper and chile. Heat for a few minutes to soften.

4 Stir in the remaining ingredients, then transfer to a food processor or blender and mix until smooth.

5 Return the soup to the saucepan and heat gently for 5–10 minutes, until hot. Garnish with a drizzle of soy cream and a sprinkling of chopped parsley and serve with the hot garlic ciabatta rolls.

baba ghanoush

This creamy eggplant dip is a favorite throughout the Middle East. The eggplants are sometimes grilled but this is not essential.

1 Preheat the oven to 400°F. Halve the eggplants lengthwise, brush the cut side with olive oil and bake for about 30 minutes, until soft.

2 Scoop out the flesh of the eggplants, transfer it to a food processor or blender, then add the remaining ingredients and blend until smooth. Transfer the mixture to a serving bowl, cover and chill until needed.

3 Just before serving, dust the purée with smoked paprika and garnish with olives and slices of lime. Serve with warm pita bread or oatcakes, and a selection of crudités for dipping.

- 2 eggplants
- 2 tablespoons olive oil
- 1 garlic clove, chopped
- juice of ½ lime
- 1 tablespoon balsamic vinegar
- 1 tablespoon vegan yogurt or soyannaise (see pages 14 and 15)
- 2½ teaspoons tahini
- 1 teaspoon ground cumin

To garnish
- smoked paprika
- olives
- slices of lime

- **4 zucchini**
- **1 tablespoon avocado or olive oil**
- **1 tablespoon soy sauce**

Pâté
- **½ cup red lentils**
- **½ onion, chopped**
- **1 garlic clove, chopped**
- **1 cup vegetable stock (see page 14)**
- **¼ cup shelled walnuts, chopped**
- **1 tablespoon rapeseed oil**
- **2½ teaspoons chopped dates**
- **1 teaspoon cider vinegar**
- **1 teaspoon yeast extract**
- **1 teaspoon soy milk**
- **1 teaspoon chopped thyme**

zucchini stuffed with lentil and walnut pâté

1 Preheat the oven to 350°F. First make the pâté. Fill a medium saucepan with cold water, add the lentils and bring to a boil.

2 Drain the lentils, rinse under running cold water, then return them to the saucepan. Add the onion, garlic and vegetable stock, bring to a boil, then simmer for 20 minutes.

3 Drain the lentils again, then stir in all the remaining pâté ingredients, transfer the mixture to a food processor or blender and mix until smooth.

4 Slice a thin sliver from the bottom of the zucchini so that they sit level on a plate. Cut a rectangle almost the length and width of the zucchini through the skin on the top side. Carefully remove the rectangle of skin, then scoop out the flesh using a teaspoon. (Freeze the flesh for use in another recipe at a later date.)

5 Mix together the avocado oil and soy sauce, then brush the cut surfaces of the zucchini with it. Bake for about 15 minutes. Remove the zucchini from the oven, fill with the lentil and walnut pâté and return to the oven for 5–10 minutes to heat through.

6 Serve with a mixed salad, red onion marmalade (see page 16) and warm oatcakes.

butter bean and pumpkin seed dip

- 1 cup cooked butter beans
- 1 garlic clove, chopped
- ¼ cup pumpkin seeds
- 2 tablespoons lime juice
- 2 tablespoons vegan yogurt (see page 14) or soy milk
- 1 tablespoon flax oil
- 1 tablespoon olive oil
- pinch of sea salt

To garnish
- 1 tablespoon chopped parsley
- 1 teaspoon cumin seeds

Healthy food rarely tasted this good in the early days of vegetarianism! In this dip, we have zinc, calcium, iron, magnesium, various B vitamins, phosphorus, potassium, omega-3 and other essential fatty acids.

1 Place all the ingredients in a food processor or blender and mix to a smooth consistency.

2 Transfer the dip to a serving bowl and garnish with the parsley and cumin seeds.

3 Serve with roasted vegetables (see page 48) or crudités, and warm pita bread or oatcakes.

smoked tofu and horseradish pâté

preparation: 7 minutes
serves: 2–4

Tofu is very versatile, and when it's smoked or marinated it takes on a life of its own. Here, with the addition of horseradish, the smoked tofu becomes almost fishy without tasting fishy.

1 Place all the ingredients in a food processor or blender and mix to a smooth consistency.

2 Transfer the pâté to a serving bowl and garnish with smoked paprika and slices of lime.

3 Serve with roasted vegetables (see page 48) or crudités, and warm pita bread or oatcakes.

- 4 oz smoked tofu
- 1 tablespoon lime juice
- 1 tablespoon flax oil
- 2 teaspoons tamarind paste
- 2 teaspoons capers
- 2 teaspoons seaweed flakes
- 1 teaspoon smoked paprika
- 1 teaspoon grated horseradish
- salt and pepper

To garnish
- smoked paprika
- slices of lime

- 1 oz arame or mixed Atlantic seaweeds
- 1 garlic clove, chopped
- 2 tablespoons lime juice
- 1 tablespoon pitted and chopped large black olives
- 1 tablespoon capers
- 1 tablespoon blackstrap molasses
- 1 tablespoon flax oil
- 1 tablespoon olive oil
- 1 tablespoon soy milk
- 1 heaping teaspoon tahini
- 1 teaspoon tamarind paste
- 1 teaspoon miso paste
- 1 teaspoon carob powder
- black pepper
- vegan cream cheese (see page 14), to serve (optional)

seaweed tapenade

The Provençal condiment on which this recipe is based contains anchovies. The seaweed used in this version has a similarly strong flavor, so use only a little at a time. It does not need salt because several of the ingredients are very salty. This tapenade makes great party food: use it to stuff cherry tomatoes or celery sticks, or mix with equal quantities of vegan cream cheese (see page 14) for canapés or as a quick snack (as illustrated).

1 Place the seaweed in a dish with the lime juice and let soak for about 30 minutes, until soft.

2 Place the softened seaweed, lime juice and all the remaining ingredients in a food processor or blender and mix to a smooth consistency.

3 Transfer the tapenade to a serving bowl, mix with cream cheese, if using, and serve with oatcakes and cherry tomatoes.

preparation: 8 minutes
cooking: 30 minutes
serves: 2

millet salad

- ½ cup millet seeds
- 1 cup vegetable stock (see page 14)
- 2 green onions, chopped
- 1 bunch of watercress, chopped
- ½ cup green beans, chopped
- ¼ cup dried apricots, chopped
- 2 tablespoons lime juice
- 1½ tablespoons chopped dried fruit
- 1½ tablespoons pumpkin seeds
- 1½ tablespoons sunflower seeds
- 2 teaspoons balsamic vinegar
- 1 teaspoon olive oil
- pinch of salt
- chopped herbs, to garnish

Despite mocking associations with bird food, millet is a good, low-allergenic, gluten-free grain; it is highly alkaline and easily digestible.

1 Place the millet seeds and vegetable stock in a small saucepan, bring to a boil and simmer for 25 minutes.

2 Rinse the millet under cold running water and drain.

3 Transfer the millet seeds to a bowl, add the remaining ingredients, then cover and chill until needed.

4 Garnish the millet with fresh herbs and serve with warm pita bread or in a tortilla wrap.

sea-fruit cocktail

preparation: 10 minutes
cooking: 25 minutes
serves: 4

Vegan prawns are available from Chinese, Thai and Korean food stores. They require no preparation before cooking. If not available, use 4 oz dried soy chunks or 8 oz smoked tofu.

1 If using dried soy chunks, boil them in water for 20 minutes with 2 tablespoons cider vinegar and 1 teaspoon salt, then allow to cool. If using smoked tofu, toss the pieces in 1 tablespoon each of soy sauce and avocado oil, and bake in a preheated oven, 350°F, for 25 minutes. Allow to cool.

2 Place the vegan prawns, soy chunks or smoked tofu in a large serving bowl, add all the remaining salad ingredients and mix well.

3 Spoon the salad mixture on to lettuce leaves and garnish with the lime, tomatoes, avocado and a sprinkling of nori flakes. Serve with warm brown bread.

- 8-oz package vegan prawns
- 8 lychees, peeled, pitted and quartered
- 1 green onion, chopped
- 1 large sweet pickle, finely chopped
- 1 garlic clove, finely chopped
- ½ cup paprika yogurt dressing (see page 16)
- 2 tablespoons capers
- 1½ tablespoons mixed Atlantic seaweed flakes or flaked nori
- 2 teaspoons chopped parsley
- ½ teaspoon smoked paprika
- pinch of sea salt

To garnish
- 1 lime, quartered
- 8 cherry tomatoes
- 2 avocados, halved, stoned, peeled and cut into fans
- nori flakes

main meals

preparation: 20 minutes
cooking: 35 minutes
serves: 4

Pizza base (see page 15)

Tomato topping
• 1 13-oz can tomatoes
• 1 onion, chopped
• 2 garlic cloves, chopped
• 1 teaspoon chopped oregano
• 1 bay leaf
• 6 mushrooms, sliced
• 1 red and 1 green pepper, seeded and chopped
• 1 carrot, grated
• ¼ cabbage, finely sliced
• 1 tablespoon olive oil
• 1 tablespoon balsamic vinegar

To garnish
• 6 canned artichoke hearts
• 6 strips baked smoked tofu
• black olives

"Cheesy" topping
• ½ cup soy milk
• ¼ cup avocado oil
• 1 tablespoon cider vinegar
• 1 boiled potato
• ¼ cup coconut oil
• 1 tablespoon tomato sauce
• 2½ teaspoons vegan bouillon powder
• 1 teaspoon Dijon mustard
• 1 teaspoon chile sauce

artichoke pizza

1 Prepare and cook the pizza base following the instructions on page 15.

2 Place the tomatoes in a food processor and blend until smooth. Transfer to a large saucepan, add the onion, garlic, oregano and bay leaf. Bring to a boil, then simmer gently for about 20 minutes.

3 Stir the remaining tomato topping ingredients into the pan, then transfer the mixture to the oiled pizza base, bringing it right up to the edges. Arrange the garnish ingredients on top, then return the pizza to the oven for 5 minutes.

4 To make the "cheesy" topping, heat the soy milk until hot but not boiling, then pour it into a food processor or blender. Add the oil and vinegar and blend well. Add the remaining "cheesy" topping ingredients, then spread the mixture over the pizza.

5 Raise the oven temperature to 400°F and bake the pizza for another 5–10 minutes, until the topping starts to bubble and turn golden brown. Serve with a crisp dressed salad.

seaweed quinoa kedgeree

- 8 oz quinoa seeds
- 2 cups vegetable stock (see page 14)
- ½ oz dried arame seaweed
- 3 tablespoons olive oil
- 1 onion, chopped
- 8 oz smoked tofu, chopped
- 1 cup avocado, roughly chopped
- 2 garlic cloves, chopped
- 2 tablespoons soy sauce
- ½ teaspoon cayenne pepper
- 1 red pepper, seeded and chopped
- ½ cup green beans, chopped
- 1 tablespoon capers
- juice of 1 lime
- 1 tablespoon chopped cilantro leaves
- salt and pepper

To garnish
- 4 sprigs of parsley
- 1 lime, cut into wedges
- nori flakes
- chile sauce (optional)
- smoked paprika

Kedgeree is a western adaptation of an Indian vegetarian rice-based dish called kitcheree, with smoked fish and boiled eggs added. These are replaced in this recipe by arame seaweed, smoked tofu and vegetables.

1 Place the quinoa and vegetable stock in a saucepan and bring to a boil. Reduce the heat, add the arame and simmer gently for 20 minutes, until the quinoa has absorbed the liquid and is light and fluffy.

2 Meanwhile, heat the oil in a frying pan and gently fry the onion and smoked tofu until the tofu begins to brown.

3 Add the avocado, garlic, soy sauce, cayenne pepper, and salt and pepper and cook, stirring, until hot.

4 Add the red pepper, beans, capers and lime juice. Stir well, then add the mixture to the pan of quinoa. Fold in the cilantro.

5 Transfer the kedgeree to a serving bowl and garnish with sprigs of parsley, wedges of lime, nori flakes, chile sauce, if using, and a sprinkling of smoked paprika. Serve with a crisp green salad.

ackee quiche

preparation: **15** minutes
cooking: **25** minutes
serves: **4**

1 Grease an 8-inch pie plate. Preheat the oven to 400°F.

2 First make the pastry. Place the flour in a bowl, add the oil and salt and mix with a fork. Add the milk and mix to make a firm dough.

3 Flour a work surface and briefly knead the dough. Roll it out and use to line the prepared pie plate. Bake for 5 minutes.

4 To make the filling, heat 2 tablespoons of the oil in a frying pan and fry the onion, mushrooms and ackees.

5 Place the yogurt, mustard, tomato purée, bouillon powder and the remaining olive oil in a small bowl and mix well.

6 Put the ackee mixture into the pie shell, spoon the yogurt mixture over the top, then garnish with the sliced tomato. Bake for 20 minutes, or until the top begins to bubble and brown.

7 Garnish the finished quiche with sprigs of parsley and a sprinkling of smoked paprika. Serve with a crisp green salad and some roasted sweet potatoes.

Pastry
- 2¼ cups self-rising wholegrain flour
- 5 tablespoons rapeseed oil
- pinch of salt
- 5 tablespoons soy milk

Filling
- 3 tablespoons olive oil
- 1 onion, chopped
- 2 cups mushrooms, chopped
- 1 8-oz can ackees, drained (see page 11)
- ½ cup vegan yogurt or soyannaise (see pages 14 and 15)
- 1 tablespoon Dijon mustard
- 2 teaspoons vegan bouillon powder
- 1 teaspoon tomato purée
- 1 large tomato, sliced

To garnish
- sprigs of parsley
- smoked paprika

Pastry

- 2⅔ cups self-rising wholegrain flour
- 1 teaspoon vegan bouillon powder
- ½ cup rapeseed oil
- ½ cup rice milk or soy milk

Filling

- 1 medium cauliflower, broken into florets
- ¼ lb asparagus, trimmed and washed
- olive oil, for oiling and frying
- 2 red onions, chopped
- 2 oz shiitake mushrooms, sliced
- ½ cup frozen sweet corn, mashed
- 1 cup sweetened soy milk
- 1 cup rapeseed oil
- juice of 1 lime
- 2 tablespoons rolled oats
- 2 tablespoons vegan tomato sauce
- scant 2 tablespoons vegan bouillon powder
- 1 tablespoon Dijon mustard
- smoked paprika
- black pepper

cauliflower and asparagus tart

1 Grease a 12 inch) tart or pie plate. Preheat the oven to 350°F.

2 To make the pastry, place the flour and bouillon powder in a bowl and rub in the oil, then mix in the milk. Knead the pastry gently for a few moments, then roll out on a floured surface and use it to line the prepared dish. Bake for 10–15 minutes, until just cooked through.

3 Meanwhile, steam the cauliflower and asparagus separately until hot but not cooked – about 4–5 minutes.

4 Heat a little olive oil in a frying pan and fry the onions and mushrooms until soft. Add the mashed sweet corn and stir until hot.

5 Heat the soy milk in a saucepan until hot but not boiling. Transfer to a food processor or blender, add the rapeseed oil, season with pepper and mix well. With the machine still running, add the lime juice and mix thoroughly to prevent curdling.

6 Add the oats, tomato sauce, bouillon powder and mustard to the milk mixture and blend again.

7 Oil the inner base of the pie crust, then spread a thin layer of the oat mixture over it. Place a layer of the mushroom mixture on top, then a layer of the cauliflower, followed by the remaining oat mixture.

8 Arrange the asparagus spears on top and sprinkle with smoked paprika. Return the tart to the oven and cook for 20 minutes. Serve with a green salad.

caribbean crumble

Filling
- 1 13-oz can tomatoes
- 2 onions, chopped
- 1 sweet potato, chopped
- 1 red and 1 green pepper, seeded and chopped
- 8 oz gungo peas, cooked
- 7 oz vegan prawns or smoked tofu, cubed
- 1 teaspoon fresh ginger, peeled and finely chopped
- ¼ teaspoon ground nutmeg
- 1 Scotch bonnet pepper, seeded and finely chopped (optional)
- salt and pepper

Crumble
- 1 cup plus 2 tablespoons wholegrain flour
- 1 cup rolled oats
- 2 tablespoons dried or freshly grated coconut
- 2 tablespoons rapeseed oil
- 2 tablespoons soy milk
- salt and pepper

To garnish
- ½ small pineapple, cored, peeled and chopped
- ½ small mango, stoned, peeled and chopped
- dried or freshly grated coconut, for coating

It's thought that the Spanish conquistadors were responsible for introducing gungo peas to Jamaica. Scotch bonnet peppers are very hot, so omit them if you dislike spicy food.

1 Preheat the oven to 350°F. Place the tomatoes in food processor or blender and mix until smooth. Transfer them to a medium saucepan, add the onions and bring to a boil, then lower the heat and simmer for 5 minutes. Add all the remaining filling ingredients to the pan and stir thoroughly.

2 Place all the dry crumble ingredients in a food processor or bowl. Add the oil and milk, season with salt and pepper and process or rub together until the mixture resembles crumbs.

3 Divide the tomato mixture between six ovenproof dishes and top evenly with the crumble. Bake for 30 minutes.

4 To serve, garnish the crumble with pieces of pineapple and mango dipped in grated coconut.

millet pastries

preparation: 20 minutes

cooking: 50 minutes

serves: 4

1 Grease a baking sheet and preheat the oven to 350°F. Place the flour and bouillon powder in a bowl, add the soy milk and oil and mix together with a fork. Knead gently for a few seconds, then cover and chill until needed.

2 Pour the millet and vegetable stock into a saucepan, bring to a boil, then simmer for 20 minutes.

3 Meanwhile, place the potato and carrot in another saucepan, add just enough water to cover, then bring to a boil and simmer for 10 minutes. Add the green beans and cauliflower and simmer for another 5 minutes. Strain the vegetables, then add to the millet along with the onion, lime juice, mustard, sage, yeast extract, bouillon powder and black pepper.

4 Divide the chilled pastry into 4 equal pieces. Flour a work surface and roll each piece into a circle about 6 inches in diameter.

5 Place a tablespoon of the millet mixture on each circle, then bring the edges of the pastry together to make a half-moon shape, and press firmly with your fingers to seal.

6 Place the pasties on the prepared baking sheet, brush them with the soyannaise and bake for 30 minutes. Serve hot with roasted vegetables (see page 48) or cold with a green salad.

Pastry
- 2¼ cups unbleached flour
- ½ teaspoon vegan bouillon powder
- ½ cup soy milk
- ⅓ cup rapeseed oil
- 1 tablespoon soyannaise (see page 15), to glaze

Filling
- ¼ cup millet seeds
- ½ cup vegetable stock (see page 14)
- 1 potato, chopped
- 1 carrot, chopped
- ½ cup green beans, chopped
- ½ cup cauliflower, chopped
- ½ onion, chopped
- juice of ½ lime
- 1 tablespoon mild mustard
- 1 teaspoon sage
- 1 teaspoon yeast extract
- 1 teaspoon vegan bouillon powder
- ½ teaspoon black pepper

preparation: 10 minutes
cooking: 30–35 minutes
serves: 4

- 1 cup amaranth (see page 11)
- 2 cups vegetable stock (see page 14)
- 8 cabbage or grapevine leaves
- 20 large black olives, pitted and quartered
- 2 pickled jalapeño peppers, chopped
- 1 garlic clove, crushed
- 1 tablespoon seaweed flakes
- 1 tablespoon pumpkin seed oil
- 2½ teaspoons balsamic vinegar
- 1 teaspoon smoked paprika
- salt and pepper
- 8 toothpicks
- avocado oil, for brushing

inca parcels

1 Preheat the oven to 350°F. Place the amaranth and vegetable stock in a medium saucepan and bring to a boil. Simmer for about 25 minutes, until the amaranth is tender and all the stock has been absorbed.

2 Meanwhile, steam the cabbage leaves for a few minutes until limp.

3 Add the olives, jalapeño peppers, garlic, seaweed flakes, pumpkin seed oil, vinegar, paprika and salt and pepper to the amaranth pan.

4 Place a tablespoonful of the mixture on each cabbage leaf, fold it into a parcel and spear with a toothpick.

5 Brush each parcel with avocado oil and bake for 5–10 minutes, until hot. Serve with a tomato, red onion and tofu salad and mixed greens.

pasta-leeky

- 8 oz gluten-free pasta
- 8 mushrooms, sliced
- 3 garlic cloves, chopped
- 2 leeks, chopped
- 4 oz tofu
- 2 cups soy or oat milk
- ½ cup frozen peas
- ½ cup shelled walnuts, chopped
- 1 bay leaf
- 1 teaspoon chopped thyme
- 2½ teaspoons cornstarch
- juice of 1 lime
- 2 teaspoons chopped cilantro leaves
- black pepper

A gluten-free pasta dish so deliciously creamy and nutty that everyone will want some. Free of oil, sugar and salt too, it's also ideal for those on a detox diet.

1 Place the pasta in a pan of cold water, bring to a boil, stir, then set aside (off the heat) with a lid on.

2 Place the mushrooms, garlic, leeks, tofu, milk, peas, walnuts, bay leaf and thyme in a large pan, bring to a boil and simmer for about 10 minutes.

3 Put the cornstarch in a small bowl, add the lime juice and stir until smooth.

4 Take the vegetables off the heat and stir in the cornstarch mixture until the sauce thickens.

5 Drain the pasta, add it to the vegetables and reheat.

6 Stir in the cilantro and black pepper, then serve in deep dishes garnished with red onion rings or apple slivers. Those not on a detox diet might like to drizzle a little hempseed oil over the top and add some salt.

tapenade and yogurt ravioli with calaloo sauce

preparation: **20** minutes
cooking: **20** minutes
serves: **2**

Calaloo is Caribbean spinach, available from West Indian grocers, usually in cans. If you can't find it, use fresh spinach instead.

1 To make the pasta, place the flours in a bowl and add the olive oil, soyannaise and salt and pepper. Mix with a fork, then knead gently until shiny and smooth. Wrap the dough in plastic wrap and chill until needed.

2 To make the sauce, heat the olive oil in a medium saucepan and fry the shallots until golden. Add the calaloo and stir until hot. Over low heat, add the cream, a little at a time, then the basil, garlic, bouillon powder and salt and pepper. Stirring constantly, add the wine. Put a large saucepan of water on to boil.

3 Break the chilled dough into 6 pieces and roll into balls. Flour a work surface and roll the balls into circles about 3¼ inches in diameter.

4 Cut each circle in half and spoon ½ teaspoon of tapenade and ½ teaspoon of yogurt slightly off-center on each one. Fold the dough over to encase the filling and make a triangular shape, moisten the edges with a little soy milk, if you like, then press the edges together to seal.

5 Place the ravioli in the pan of boiling water and simmer for about 10 minutes, until hot. Drain and serve with the calaloo sauce, sprinkle with pepper and garnish with basil. A crisp green salad makes a good accompaniment.

Pasta
- ½ cup semolina flour
- ½ cup bread flour
- 1 tablespoon olive oil
- 1 tablespoon soyannaise (see page 15)
- 6 teaspoons vegan tapenade or pesto
- 6 teaspoons vegan yogurt (see page 14)
- soy milk (optional)
- salt and pepper

Calaloo sauce
- 1 tablespoon olive oil
- 2 shallots, chopped
- 1 9-oz can calaloo, drained, or 8 oz spinach, chopped
- ⅓ cup soy or coconut cream
- 4 basil leaves, chopped
- 1 garlic clove, crushed
- 2 teaspoons vegan bouillon powder
- ¼ cup dry white vegan wine, or half and half lemon juice and water
- salt and pepper
- basil leaves, to garnish

preparation: **20** minutes

cooking: **1 ¾** hours

serves: **6**

- 1 cup dried chestnuts
- 4 cups vegetable stock (see page 14)
- 1½ lbs potatoes, chopped
- 1 sweet potato, chopped
- 1 tablespoon olive oil
- 6 tomatoes, chopped
- 2 onions, chopped
- 1 carrot, chopped
- 1 green pepper, seeded and chopped
- 1 small zucchini, chopped
- 1 cup cauliflower, chopped
- ½ cup frozen peas
- 1 tablespoon chopped dates
- 1 tablespoon yeast extract
- 6 sprigs of rosemary, leaves only, finely chopped
- 3 tablespoons sweetened soy milk
- 1 tablespoon chopped parsley
- 1 heaping tablespoon cornstarch
- 1 teaspoon carob powder
- 2 tablespoons orange juice
- 1 tablespoon balsamic vinegar
- 2½ teaspoons tomato purée
- 1 teaspoon blackstrap molasses
- salt and pepper

chestnut cottage pies

A lovely winter warmer, this recipe uses individual pie dishes, but you could use one large pie dish if you prefer. The chestnuts absorb the flavors of the other ingredients, while adding their own nutty sweetness.

1 Cover the dried chestnuts with the stock and soak overnight, or boil them in the stock for 1 hour.

2 Place the potatoes and sweet potato in a pan of water, bring to a boil, then simmer until soft – about 25 minutes.

3 Meanwhile, heat the olive oil in a pan and add the tomatoes, all the remaining vegetables, the dates, yeast extract and rosemary. Add this mixture to the chestnuts and their liquid, much of which the chestnuts will have absorbed, and simmer for 15–20 minutes.

4 Preheat the oven to 350°F. Drain the potatoes and mash them with the soy milk. Stir in the parsley, plus some salt and pepper.

5 Place the cornstarch and carob powder in a small bowl, add the orange juice, vinegar, tomato purée and molasses, and mix into a paste. Add the paste to the chestnut mixture, then stir over low heat until the liquid thickens.

6 Divide the chestnut mixture equally between six 5-inch individual pie plates. Place a layer of mashed potatoes on top and bake for about 20 minutes, until lightly browned.

jamaican patties

Pastry
- 2 cups unbleached flour
- 2 teaspoons curry powder
- 1 teaspoon baking powder
- ½ teaspoon salt
- ¼ cup coconut oil
- ¼ cup rapeseed oil
- ½ cup cold rice milk or soy milk, plus more for brushing

Filling
- 2 tablespoons chilled, solidified coconut oil
- 6 oz sweet potato, finely chopped
- 3 oz cassava, peeled and finely chopped (see page 11)
- 1 red onion, finely chopped
- 4 oz tofu, mashed
- 1 cup chestnut mushrooms, finely chopped
- ¼ cup frozen peas
- 1 teaspoon chopped thyme
- 1 teaspoon curry powder
- ¼ teaspoon nutmeg
- salt and pepper

1 Place the flour, curry powder, baking powder and salt in a large bowl. Rub in the coconut oil, then stir in the rapeseed oil with a fork until the mixture resembles coarse breadcrumbs. Add just enough rice milk to make a dough that holds together. Wrap the dough in plastic wrap and chill for at least 30 minutes.

2 To make the filling, heat the coconut oil in a large frying pan. Add the sweet potato and cassava and fry over medium heat until they start to soften and brown. Add the onion and tofu and continue to cook, stirring, until they too start to brown. Stir in all the remaining ingredients, then cover and simmer for 5–10 minutes, until the sweet potato is cooked right through. Transfer the mixture to a plate and allow to cool.

3 Preheat the oven to 400°F. Grease 2 baking sheets. Flour a work surface and roll out the chilled pastry to a thickness of ¼ inch.

4 Cut twelve 4-inch circles out of the pastry. Spoon the filling equally onto the circles. Moisten the edges of the pastry with a little rice milk, then fold them over to make half-moon shapes and press the edges together with a fork.

5 Place the patties on the prepared baking sheets, brush with the remaining rice milk and prick the top of each patty with a fork. Bake for about 30 minutes, until the crust is golden brown. Serve with a rice salad or mashed potatoes and beans.

vegetable kebabs with satay sauce

preparation: 25 minutes
cooking: 30 minutes
serves: 4

These tasty kebabs can be grilled, baked or barbecued, but it's important to soak the kebab sticks first so that they don't burn.

1 Soak 8 wooden satay or kebab sticks in cold water for at least 20 minutes. Preheat the oven to 350°F.

2 Pour the lime juice, molasses, soy sauce, chile sauce and oil into a large bowl and mix well. Add the tofu and all the prepared fruits and vegetables, and stir until thoroughly coated.

3 Thread chunks of tofu, fruit and vegetables onto the soaked kebab sticks, alternating ingredients to give a range of color and texture. Place on a baking sheet and bake for 30 minutes, or grill or barbecue until browned on all sides.

4 Meanwhile, prepare the sauce. Heat the oil in a medium pan, add the onion and fry gently until soft. Add the remaining sauce ingredients, stirring constantly until the peanut butter melts and the mixture is hot.

5 Serve the kebabs on a bed of brown basmati rice or stir-fried rice noodles with the satay sauce poured over the top.

- 2 tablespoons lime juice
- 1 tablespoon blackstrap molasses
- 1 tablespoon soy sauce
- 1 tablespoon sweet chile sauce
- 1 tablespoon avocado oil
- 4 oz tofu, cubed
- 1 tart apple, quartered
- 4 pineapple chunks
- 4 mango chunks
- 4 tomatoes, halved horizontally
- 1 red onion, quartered
- 8 mushrooms, halved
- 1 red and 1 green pepper, seeded and quartered
- 1 sweet corn cob, cooked and sliced into 8 rounds
- 1 sweet potato, boiled and thickly sliced
- 1 zucchini, thickly sliced

Sauce
- 1 tablespoon coconut oil
- 1 onion, finely chopped
- 1 garlic clove, chopped
- ½ cup peanut butter
- ¼ cup creamed coconut
- 3 tablespoons soy milk
- 2 tablespoons lime juice
- 2 tablespoons soy sauce
- 2 tablespoons blackstrap molasses
- 1 tablespoon sweet chile sauce
- 1 teaspoon ground cumin

preparation: 15 minutes
cooking: 30 minutes
serves: 4

- 2 medium potatoes, chopped
- 1 lemongrass stalk
- ¼ cup lentils
- 1 tablespoon coconut oil
- 6 mushrooms, sliced
- 2 garlic cloves, chopped
- 1 onion, chopped
- 1 teaspoon turmeric
- 1 teaspoon ground cumin
- 1 yellow pepper, seeded and chopped
- 1 zucchini, chopped
- 1 cup frozen sweet corn
- 1 cup coconut milk
- ½ cup green beans
- juice of 1 lime
- 1 tablespoon chopped cilantro leaves

mild coconut curry

1 Put the potatoes, lemongrass and lentils into a medium saucepan and add enough boiling water to just cover the tops of the potatoes. Return to a boil, then simmer for about 15 minutes.

2 Heat the oil in a large saucepan and fry the mushrooms, garlic, onion, turmeric and cumin until the onion is soft. Add all the remaining ingredients except for the cilantro and stir well.

3 Remove the lemongrass from the lentil pan, then add the lentil mixture to the onion mixture.

4 Simmer everything for about 10 minutes, or until the lentils are soft, then add the chopped cilantro.

5 Serve with brown basmati rice cooked with a few cardamom pods, plus warm naan bread made without milk or yogurt.

wild mushroom and pine nut phyllo baskets

preparation: 15 minutes
cooking: 15 minutes
serves: 2

- 4 tablespoons avocado oil
- 1 red onion, chopped
- 12 oz oyster mushrooms, stalks finely chopped, tops trimmed
- ¼ cup pine nuts
- 3 garlic cloves, 1 crushed and 2 chopped
- ¼ cup vegetable stock (see page 14)
- 2 tablespoons brandy or whiskey
- 1 tablespoon soy sauce
- 4 12-inch sheets of phyllo pastry
- ½ cup soy cream or vegan yogurt (see page 14)
- 1 tablespoon sweet chile sauce, plus extra for drizzling
- 1 tablespoon maple syrup (optional)
- 1 lime, sliced, to garnish (optional)

Try to find red oyster mushrooms for this recipe, because they are full of flavor.

1 Preheat the oven to 350°F. Heat 2 tablespoons of the oil in a medium saucepan and fry the onion, mushrooms, pine nuts and crushed garlic until golden brown. Stir in the brandy, vegetable stock and soy sauce, then remove from the heat and set aside.

2 Take 1 sheet of phyllo pastry and lightly brush the surface with some of the remaining oil. Place another sheet on top and brush with oil. Cut the double thickness in half, place one half in a diamond shape over the square half below. This will make a star shape with 8 points.

3 Drape the prepared pastry over a small baking potato wrapped in foil. Brush the pastry with oil and place on a baking sheet. Repeat steps 2 and 3 until you have the basis of 4 phyllo baskets. Bake the phyllo baskets for about 10 minutes, until crisp and golden.

4 Stir 6 tablespoons of the soy cream into the mushrooms, followed by the chopped garlic, chile sauce and maple syrup, if using. Return to a simmer.

5 Carefully lift the phyllo baskets from their supports, then fill with the mushroom mixture. Discard the potatoes or continue to bake them as normal and use them for another recipe. Add drizzles of the remaining soy cream and sweet chile sauce to each basket and garnish with a slice of lime, if you like. Serve with steamed peas and brown basmati rice.

enchiladas with mushroom and sweet corn filling

preparation: 15 minutes
cooking: 40 minutes
serves: 4

- 4 vegan corn tortillas

Filling
- 1 tablespoon olive oil
- 1 red onion, chopped
- 4 chestnut mushrooms, chopped
- ¼ cup textured soy protein
- 1 carrot, grated
- 1 garlic clove, chopped
- ½ green pepper, seeded and chopped
- juice of ½ lime
- 1 cup tomato and orange soup (see page 58)
- ½ cup cooked kidney beans
- ½ cup sweet corn
- 1 tablespoon ground almonds
- 1 teaspoon chopped green chiles
- 1 teaspoon each cumin, parsley and ground coriander
- 1 teaspoon yeast extract
- black pepper

Sauce
- 1 cup sweetened soy milk
- 2 tablespoons potato flour
- 2 scant tablespoons coconut oil
- 1 tablespoon vegan bouillon powder
- 1 tablespoon Dijon mustard
- 1 heaping tablespoon cornstarch
- ½ teaspoon grated nutmeg

1 Grease a roasting pan and preheat the oven to 400°F.

2 To make the filling, heat the olive oil in a medium saucepan and fry the onion, mushrooms and textured soy protein for 5 minutes until soft. Stir in all the remaining filling ingredients with scant ½ cup water and simmer for about 10 minutes.

3 Heat the tortillas according to the package instructions and keep them warm while making the sauce, interleaving them with sheets of wax paper so they don't stick together.

4 Place all the sauce ingredients in a small saucepan and heat until the mixture thickens.

5 Put 2 tablespoons of the filling on each tortilla, roll them up and put them in the prepared roasting pan, seam side down. Spoon any remaining filling over the tortillas, then pour the sauce over them. Bake for 20 minutes until they start to bubble and brown.

6 Serve the enchiladas with a salad of red cabbage and red onions.

haggis and mashed root vegetables

Haggis
- 1 lb rutabaga, turnip or squash, finely chopped
- 1 teaspoon fresh ginger, peeled and finely chopped
- ¼ cup coconut oil
- 1⅛ cups rolled oats
- 4 mushrooms, chopped
- 1 onion, chopped
- 1 carrot, finely chopped
- 1 cup cooked kidney beans, chopped
- ½ cup shelled walnuts, chopped
- 2 tablespoons rapeseed oil
- 2 tablespoons lime juice
- 1 tablespoon soy sauce
- 1 tablespoon Scotch whisky or balsamic vinegar
- 3 teaspoons yeast extract
- 2 teaspoons black pepper
- 1 teaspoon chopped parsley
- 1 teaspoon chopped thyme
- 1 teaspoon chopped sage
- ½ teaspoon cayenne pepper
- ½ teaspoon ground nutmeg

Potato mash
- 1¼ lbs potatoes, quartered
- 2½ tablespoons vegan margarine
- 1 tablespoon soy cream
- ½ teaspoon chopped rosemary
- salt and pepper

1 Preheat the oven to 350°F. Place three-fourths of the rutabaga in a large saucepan of water, add the fresh ginger, bring to a boil and simmer for 30 minutes. Put the potatoes for the mash in another large saucepan of cold water, bring to a boil and simmer for 30 minutes, until soft.

2 Meanwhile, heat 2 tablespoons of the coconut oil in a large nonstick frying pan and gently toast the oats for about 2 minutes, stirring constantly, until golden brown. Transfer to a bowl and set aside.

3 Heat the remaining coconut oil, then gently fry the remaining rutabaga with the mushrooms, onion and carrot for about 10 minutes until the rutabaga starts to soften. Add the kidney beans and stir until hot. Transfer the fried vegetables to the bowl of oats, then add all the remaining haggis ingredients.

4 Divide the mixture between four 3¼-inch ovenproof ramekins, cover with foil and place in a deep roasting pan half-filled with boiling water. Bake for 30 minutes.

5 Reheat the boiled rutabaga, then drain and mash with half the margarine and salt and pepper. Reheat the boiled potatoes, then drain and mash with the soy cream, the remaining margarine and the rosemary.

6 Remove the ramekins from the oven, run a sharp knife around the edge of each one, then turn out on to warmed plates. Add 2 spoonfuls of each mash to the plates. Serve this vegan version of the traditional Scottish sheep's sausage with a tot of Scotch whisky.

sunday roasted drumsticks

preparation: 10 minutes
cooking: 30 minutes
serves: 2

The perfect choice for a festive dinner or a long, lazy Sunday lunch, these drumsticks are best served with rich gravy and red wine. Or, if you want an al fresco meal, press them around a wooden stick and serve at a summer picnic.

1 Grease a baking sheet and preheat the oven to 400°F. Place all the ingredients except the coconut oil in a bowl.

2 Melt the coconut oil and stir into the chestnut mixture to make a dough. Mold the dough into whatever shapes you like. (Drumsticks are good for Sunday lunch or picnics.)

3 Place the shapes on the prepared baking sheet and bake for 30 minutes, turning once.

4 Serve the drumsticks with roasted potatoes, broccoli drizzled with hemp oil, carrots cooked in orange juice, steamed Brussels sprouts and cranberry sauce.

- 14-oz can butter beans, drained and mashed
- 8-oz can chestnuts, drained and mashed
- 3 tablespoons dried textured vegetable protein rehydrated in ½ cup hot vegetable stock (see page 14), or 3 heaping tablespoons crumbled smoked tofu
- 3 tablespoons dry sage and onion stuffing mix
- juice of ½ lime
- 2½ teaspoons herbes de Provence
- 2 heaping tablespoons coconut oil
- salt and pepper

- 5 cups vegetable stock (see page 14)
- pinch of saffron threads (optional)
- 2 bay leaves
- 1 oz dried porcini mushrooms, broken into pieces
- 2 scant tablespoons dried arame seaweed, crushed
- 3 teaspoons vegan bouillon powder
- 2 tablespoons coconut oil
- 1 tablespoon avocado oil
- 2 garlic cloves, finely chopped
- 1 small onion, finely chopped
- 1½ cups arborio rice
- 2 cups dry white wine
- ½ cup frozen peas
- ¼ cup toasted pine nuts
- ¼ cup ground almonds
- 1 tablespoon chopped basil
- salt and pepper
- hemp oil, to serve

arame almond risotto

1 Pour the vegetable stock into a large saucepan, bring to a boil, then reduce to a simmer. Add the saffron, if using, bay leaves, mushrooms, arame and 1 teaspoon of the bouillon powder, stir and let simmer.

2 Heat the 1 tablespoon of the coconut oil and the avocado oil in a large frying pan, add the garlic and onion and fry gently until translucent. Pour the rice into the pan and fry for about 5 minutes without browning.

3 When the rice is crackling hot, add ½ cup of hot stock and stir for 2–3 minutes. When the rice has absorbed that liquid, add 1 cup of stock and stir again until absorbed.

4 Add the wine, ½ cup at a time, and continue stirring and cooking the risotto over low heat. When a spoon drawn through the rice leaves a clear, dry wake behind it, add more stock.

5 Continue in this way until the risotto is thoroughly cooked — the rice grains should be firm to the bite. Then stir in the remaining coconut oil plus the peas, pine nuts and salt and pepper.

6 Remove the bay leaves from the remaining stock, then pour the stock, plus the arame and mushrooms, into the rice. Take the rice off the heat, stir thoroughly, then cover and let stand for 5 minutes.

7 Gently warm the ground almonds in a hot oven for a few minutes, then mix with the remaining bouillon powder. Stir the basil into the risotto, then transfer to a warmed serving dish. Sprinkle with the ground almonds and a drizzle of hemp oil.

- 2 tablespoons olive oil
- 2 small onions, chopped
- 1 small pumpkin or squash, seeded and chopped
- 1 teaspoon turmeric
- 1 teaspoon paprika
- 1 teaspoon cinnamon
- 2 carrots, grated
- ½ red pepper, seeded and chopped
- 2 tablespoons pitted dried plums, chopped
- 1 tablespoon blackstrap molasses
- zest and juice of 1 orange
- 1 lb vegan shortcrust pastry
- 2 tablespoons ground almonds
- 2 tablespoons ground pumpkin seeds
- ½ cup soy milk
- ½ cup rapeseed oil
- juice of 1 lime
- 1 tablespoon Dijon mustard

savory pumpkin pie

Like many squashes, pumpkin has a subtle flavor, so it can be mixed with a variety of other ingredients to make both sweet and savory dishes.

1 Grease a 12-inch pie plate. Preheat the oven to 400°F. Heat 1 tablespoon of the olive oil in a large saucepan and gently fry the onions, pumpkin, turmeric, paprika and cinnamon until the pumpkin is soft. Add the carrots, red pepper, dried plums, molasses and orange zest and juice, stir until hot, then remove from the heat.

2 Roll out the pastry on a floured surface and use to line the prepared pie plate. Reserve the trimmings.

3 Mix the ground almonds and pumpkin seeds and sprinkle them on the pastry base. Spread the pumpkin mixture on top of the seed mixture.

4 Heat the soy milk until almost boiling, then add the rapeseed oil, mixing well with a handheld blender. With the blender running, gradually add the lime juice, then the mustard. Spread the mixture on top of the pie.

5 Roll out the pastry trimmings on a floured surface and cut into ½-inch wide strips. Weave them on top of the pie to create a lattice effect. Brush the pastry with the remaining olive oil and bake the pie for 30 minutes.

6 Serve the pie hot with baked beans and mashed potatoes and a green salad.

sea-fruit strudel

preparation: 20 minutes

cooking: 40 minutes

serves: 6

1 Preheat the oven to 400°F. Place the seaweed in a bowl and sprinkle with the lime juice. Lightly brush the phyllo sheets with avocado oil and arrange in 2 piles on sheets of parchment paper at least 2 inches bigger all around.

2 Heat 2 tablespoons of the avocado oil in a large nonstick frying pan and gently fry the onion, eggplant, mushrooms and mustard seeds. Add the red pepper and the seaweed with the lime juice and simmer until all the juices have been absorbed. Remove from the heat and mix in the remaining ingredients.

3 Divide the mixture equally between the 2 piles of phyllo, spreading it evenly over the surface and leaving a 1½-inch gap along the edge farthest from you.

4 Using the parchment paper, gently roll the pastry into a log shape and press along the empty edge to seal. With the strudels still sitting on the paper, gently lift them on to a baking sheet, ensuring that the seal is underneath. You might have to bend them to fit, but that gives a nice wrinkled effect.

5 Cut off the excess paper, then brush the strudels with the remaining oil and sprinkle with sesame seeds. Bake for 30 minutes until crisp and golden. When ready, cut into slices and serve with a spicy rice salad and curly kale tossed in oil and crushed garlic.

- 1 oz mixed Atlantic seaweed
- juice of 2 limes
- 1 16-oz package phyllo pastry (large sheets)
- 5 tablespoons avocado oil
- 1 red onion, chopped
- 1 small eggplant, chopped
- ½ cup mushrooms, chopped
- 1 teaspoon brown mustard seeds
- ½ red pepper, seeded and chopped
- 1 tart apple, cored and chopped
- zest of 1 orange
- ¼ cup dried apricots, chopped
- ¼ cup chopped hazelnuts
- ¼ cup pine nuts
- 1 tablespoon capers
- 1 tablespoon miso
- ½ teaspoon cayenne pepper
- black pepper
- 1 tablespoon sesame seeds, to garnish

preparation: 15 minutes
cooking: 40–45 minutes
serves: 4

Dumplings

- ½ cup brown basmati rice
- ¼ cup wild rice
- ¼ cup lentils
- 2 cups vegetable stock (see page 14)
- ½ cup self-rising wholegrain flour
- 1 tablespoon dried coconut
- 2½ teaspoons dried seaweed flakes
- 1 garlic clove, finely chopped
- 1 teaspoon cumin
- 1 teaspoon chopped mint
- ¼ cup coconut oil

Tomato sauce

- 1 tablespoon olive oil
- 1 red onion, chopped
- 4 tomatoes, chopped
- 1 red pepper, seeded and chopped
- 1 small red chile, finely chopped (optional)
- 1 tablespoon arrowroot
- juice of ½ lime
- 1 tablespoon blackstrap molasses
- 1 tablespoon balsamic vinegar
- 1 teaspoon salt
- black pepper, to taste

wild rice and lentil dumplings in tomato sauce

1 Place the rice and lentils in a large saucepan, add 2 cups of water, bring to the boil and simmer for 5 minutes. Drain, rinse well, then return them to the pan.

2 Add the vegetable stock, bring to a boil and simmer for 15–20 minutes, until the rice is cooked (not all of the stock may be absorbed).

3 Meanwhile, make the tomato sauce. Heat the olive oil in a small saucepan and gently fry the onion until soft. Add the tomatoes, red pepper and chile to the pan and simmer for about 10 minutes.

4 Grease a baking sheet and preheat the oven to 350°F. Drain the rice and lentils, place in a mixing bowl and add the flour, coconut, seaweed, garlic, cumin, mint and salt and pepper.

5 Using 2 spoons dipped in warm water to prevent sticking, shape the lentil mixture into ovals the size of an egg and place them on the prepared baking sheet. Top each dumpling with a knob of coconut oil and bake for about 20 minutes, turning and basting occasionally, until golden and crispy all over.

6 Place the tomato mixture in a food processor or blender and mix until smooth. Mix together the arrowroot and lime juice and add to the sauce. With the machine still running, add the molasses, vinegar and salt and pepper, then return the sauce to the pan and simmer until the mixture thickens.

7 To serve, put the crispy dumplings into warmed bowls and pour over the tomato sauce. A crisp green side salad makes a good accompaniment.

rice noodle and vegetable stir-fry

- 2 oz rice noodles
- 2½ teaspoons coconut oil
- 1 red onion, sliced
- 8 oz rehydrated soy chunks or tofu
- 2 tablespoons soy sauce
- 8 lychees, peeled, pitted and quartered
- 1 garlic clove, finely chopped
- 1 cup finely sliced cabbage
- 1 cup bean sprouts
- 2½ teaspoons blackstrap molasses
- 1 teaspoon fresh ginger, peeled and finely chopped

To serve
- nori flakes
- sesame seeds
- lime wedges (optional)

1 Soak the rice noodles in boiling water for 4 minutes, then rinse in cold water and drain.

2 Heat a wok or large frying pan until very hot, add the coconut oil, then the onion and soy. Stir briskly to sear on all sides until golden.

3 Pour in the soy sauce and stir to coat the mixture.

4 Reduce the heat and add the remaining ingredients plus the drained noodles, stirring until hot.

5 Transfer the stir-fry to warmed serving bowls, sprinkle with the nori flakes and sesame seeds, and serve with a wedges of lime, if desired.

spicy basmati salad

- 1 cup brown basmati rice, rinsed
- ½ cup lentils, rinsed
- 3½ cups vegetable stock (see page 14)
- 2 tablespoons olive oil
- 2 small onions, chopped
- 6 chestnut mushrooms, finely chopped
- 4 garlic cloves, minced
- 2 tablespoons curry paste
- ½ cup apple juice
- juice of 1 lime
- 2 tablespoons golden raisins
- 2½ teaspoons mango chutney
- 1 teaspoon vegan bouillon powder
- 2 tomatoes, finely chopped
- 1 red pepper, seeded and finely chopped
- ½ cup sweet corn
- coconut flakes and sprigs of cilantro, to serve

1 Place the rice, lentils and vegetable stock in a saucepan, bring to a boil and simmer for 20 minutes, until almost cooked.

2 Meanwhile, heat the olive oil in a large saucepan and gently fry the onions until soft. Add the mushrooms and garlic and cook until soft.

3 Stir in the curry paste and heat through. Add the apple and lime juices, raisins, chutney and bouillon powder, stir well and simmer for 3 minutes.

4 Drain the rice and lentils and add to the curry mixture. Stir in the tomatoes, red pepper and sweet corn, then simmer for 10 minutes until the juices are absorbed and the rice is completely tender.

5 Serve sprinkled with coconut flakes and sprigs of cilantro. Roasted vegetables (see page 48) and a mixed salad are good accompaniments.

walnut and mushroom pie

preparation: 20 minutes
cooking: 40–45 minutes
serves: 6

When stewed in gravy, walnuts develop a velvety richness. They are said to be good for the kidneys, lubricating the digestive system and improving the metabolism.

1 Grease a 12-inch pie plate or six 4-inch individual dishes. Preheat the oven to 350°F.

2 Place the tomatoes in a food processor or blender and mix to a purée. Transfer the purée to a large saucepan and bring to a boil, then reduce the heat to a simmer. Add the carrot, onion, red pepper, mushrooms, walnuts, dates and mustard powder, stir well, then cover and simmer for 15 minutes.

3 Meanwhile, flour a work surface, cut the pastry in half and roll out to a ¼-inch thickness. Use to line the prepared dish or dishes, arrange parchment paper over the pastry and place some pie weights on top, then bake for 7 minutes.

4 Combine all the remaining ingredients in a small bowl and gradually pour into the stew, stirring constantly as it thickens.

5 Spoon the stew into the pie crust. Roll out the remaining pastry and use to cover the pie(s).

6 Brush the pastry with soyannaise, sprinkle with the sesame seeds and bake the pie(s) for 25–30 minutes, until puffed and golden. Serve with mashed potatoes and steamed vegetables drizzled with oil.

- 1 8-oz can tomatoes
- 1 carrot, finely chopped
- 1 red onion, chopped
- 1 red pepper, seeded and chopped
- 3 cups oyster mushrooms, sliced
- 1 cup shelled walnuts
- 1 tablespoon chopped dates
- 1 teaspoon mustard powder
- 1 lb vegan puff pastry
- 2 tablespoons rapeseed oil
- 1 tablespoon vegan gravy powder or cornstarch
- 1 tablespoon balsamic vinegar
- 1 tablespoon chopped parsley
- 2½ teaspoons yeast extract
- 1 teaspoon carob powder
- 1 teaspoon black pepper
- 1 tablespoon soyannaise (see page 15), to glaze
- 2½ teaspoons sesame seeds, to garnish

mushroom stew with herb dumplings

preparation: 25 minutes
cooking: 45 minutes
serves: 4

- 1 potato, chopped
- ½ cup lentils
- 1 oz dried shiitake mushrooms, broken into pieces
- 2 cups vegetable stock (see page 14)
- 1 red onion, chopped
- 1 carrot, chopped
- 1 red pepper, seeded and chopped
- 1 cup oyster mushrooms, sliced
- 1 cup chopped cabbage
- ½ cup frozen peas
- 2 heaping teaspoons cornstarch
- 2 teaspoons carob powder
- 2 teaspoons vegan bouillon powder
- ½ cup vegan sherry
- 2 tablespoons vegan tomato sauce
- 1 tablespoon molasses
- 1 teaspoon yeast extract

Dumplings
- 1½ cups self-rising wholegrain flour
- ½ cup soy milk
- ¼ cup rapeseed oil
- 1 teaspoon vegan bouillon powder
- 1 teaspoon chopped sage
- 1 teaspoon chopped thyme
- 1 teaspoon chopped parsley

1 Place the potato, shiitake mushrooms and lentils in a large saucepan, add the stock and 1 cup water and bring to a boil. Reduce the heat and simmer for 20 minutes.

2 Put all the dumpling ingredients in a food processor, mix well, then divide the mixture into 12 balls.

3 Add the remaining vegetables to the potato mixture.

4 Place the cornstarch, carob powder and bouillon powder in a mixing bowl, add the sherry, tomato sauce, molasses and yeast extract and stir until smooth. Gradually add this mixture to the vegetables, stirring constantly as the stew thickens.

5 Place the dumplings on top of the stew, replace the lid and simmer gently for about another 20 minutes, until the dumplings are cooked. (If you prefer, you can cook the stew and dumplings in a casserole dish, covered, in a preheated oven at 350°F.)

preparation: 10 minutes
cooking: 1¼ hours
serves: 6

- 1 cup millet
- 2 cups vegetable stock (see page 14)
- 1 4-inch piece of lemongrass
- 1 slice of fresh ginger, peeled
- 2 tablespoons olive oil
- 1 red onion, chopped
- 1 carrot, grated
- 1 garlic clove, chopped
- ½ oz dried shiitake mushrooms, ground (use an herb mill or a coffee grinder)
- ¼ cup pumpkin seeds, ground
- 2½ teaspoons carob powder
- 2½ teaspoons balsamic vinegar
- 2½ teaspoons soy sauce
- 2 teaspoons chopped thyme
- 1 teaspoon yeast extract
- 1 tablespoon coconut oil, for greasing
- salt and pepper

millet burgers

These succulent burgers can be served in the traditional way or allowed to become cold, then marinated in a mixture of soy sauce and olive oil with a dash of balsamic vinegar and grilled. They can also be used cold in sandwiches with pickles or put into pita bread with some crisp greens and chile sauce.

1 Preheat the oven to 350°F. Place the millet in a saucepan, add the stock and bring to a boil. Reduce the heat, add the lemongrass and ginger, and simmer for about 30 minutes, until the liquid has been absorbed.

2 Meanwhile, heat the olive oil in a frying pan and gently fry the onion until beginning to brown.

3 Once the millet is cooked, discard the ginger and lemongrass, then add the onion and all the remaining ingredients.

4 Grease a baking sheet with the coconut oil, then put spoonfuls of the millet mixture on it, flattening them out to about 3 inches in diameter and ½-inch thick.

5 Bake the burgers for about 40 minutes, turning them halfway through. They should be firm and succulent. Serve in buns with sauerkraut and a crisp green salad.

chapter four

desserts

preparation: 15 minutes
cooking: 25–35 minutes
serves: 8–10 brownies

- 2¼ cups wholegrain flour
- 1 cup rice milk or water
- ¼ cup soy milk
- ¼ cup rapeseed oil
- 3 tablespoons cocoa powder
- 1 tablespoon carob powder
- 1 cup dark brown sugar
- ½ cup dried plums, pitted
- ¼ cup medjool dates, pitted
- 1 teaspoon salt
- 1 teaspoon vanilla extract
- 1½ teaspoons baking powder
- 1 tablespoon ground almonds

date and dried plum brownies

1 Line an 8 x 8 inch baking pan with parchment paper and oil lightly. Preheat the oven to 350°F.

2 Place 2 heaping tablespoons of the flour in a saucepan and mix in the rice milk. Cook, stirring constantly, over medium heat until thick. Set aside to cool completely.

3 Combine the soy milk, oil, cocoa and carob in a bowl and stir until smooth.

4 Transfer the cooled flour mixture to a food processer or blender, add the sugar, plums, dates, salt and vanilla and blend until smooth. Add the cocoa mixture and blend again.

5 Mix the remaining flour with the baking powder and the ground almonds, then add to the plum mixture and blend again. Pour the mixture into the prepared pan and bake for 25–35 minutes, until firm to the touch.

6 Cut into slices and serve hot with a scoop of vegan ice cream and some grated vegan chocolate.

preparation: 10 minutes
cooking: 23 minutes
serves: 6

lime soufflettes

- 2 limes
- 1 cup sweetened soy milk
- 4 heaping tablespoons confectioner's sugar
- 1 cup rapeseed oil
- slices of lime, to decorate (optional)

This vegan recipe is, of course, made without eggs or cream, so to call it a soufflé would be regarded as culinary treason in some parts of the world. However, it's so creamy and zesty that it would be a great shame to go through life without enjoying a spoonful.

1 Preheat the oven to 400°F. Zest the rind from one of the limes and squeeze the juice from both.

2 Heat the soy milk with the sugar until hot but not boiling. Transfer the mixture to a food processor or blender, add the oil and blend briefly. Gradually add the lime juice, whisking constantly to avoid curdling.

3 Stir in the lime zest, then pour the mixture into six 3¼-inch ramekins and bake for 20 minutes until the soufflettes have risen just above the rims of the ramekins.

4 Allow to cool, then serve with strawberries or slices of mango and some scoops of vegan ice cream. Decorate with slices of lime, if you like.

moist chocolate crumb cake

preparation: 15 minutes, plus cooling
cooking: 45 minutes
serves: 8

1 Preheat the oven to 350°F. Crush the graham crackers, then pour them into a small saucepan and heat gently with the coconut oil and soy milk for a few minutes, stirring, until well combined.

2 Using the back of a spoon, press the crumb mixture into the bottom of a 12-inch tart pan or into eight 3¼-inch ramekins.

3 Place all the remaining ingredients in a bowl and combine with a handheld mixer or blender.

4 Pour the tofu mixture on top of the crumb base, then bake for 45 minutes. Allow to cool for 2 hours before serving.

5 Decorate with crystallized ginger and nasturtium leaves, then serve with a spoonful of ice cream and a drizzle of maple syrup.

- 12 vegan graham crackers
- 2 tablespoons coconut oil
- 2 tablespoons soy milk
- 8 oz silken tofu
- 1 banana
- ½ cup maple syrup
- ¼ cup cocoa powder
- 3 tablespoons orange juice
- 2 tablespoons tahini
- 2 tablespoons raisins
- 1 tablespoon lime juice
- 2 teaspoons arrowroot
- 2 teaspoons vanilla extract
- pinch of salt

To decorate
- crystallized ginger
- nasturtium leaves

chocolate chip and walnut ice cream

- 4 oz dairy-free dark chocolate (70 percent cocoa solids)
- 1 tablespoon chopped walnuts
- 1 cup coconut cream
- ½ cup soy milk
- ¼ cup dates, chopped
- ¼ cup dried apricots, chopped
- 2 tablespoons mixed dried fruit
- 2 tablespoons agave or maple syrup
- 2 tablespoons lime juice
- 2 tablespoons essential seed mix (see page 20)
- 2 tablespoons flax oil
- 2 tablespoons rolled oats
- 1 tablespoon Cointreau
- 1 tablespoon vegan yogurt (see page 14)
- 1 tablespoon vegan margarine
- 2 teaspoons carob powder

Is there a more delicious way of getting your daily dose of essential omega-3 than a scoop of this soft-set ice cream? We don't think so. Try it with chocolate chip cookies (see page 124).

1 Break the chocolate into pieces, then place 3 oz of it in a heatproof bowl over a saucepan of simmering water and heat until melted. (Do not let the bowl touch the water.)

2 Chop the remaining chocolate into chip-sized pieces, mix with the walnuts and set aside.

3 Place all the remaining ingredients in a bowl and use a handheld mixer to combine until quite smooth. Stir the melted chocolate into the fruit mixture, then mix in the walnuts and chocolate chips.

4 Transfer the mixture to a suitable lidded container and place in the freezer for 1 hour. Remove from the freezer and break up the mixture with a fork to reduce the ice crystals. Repeat this process every hour for the next 4 hours.

5 If frozen for longer than 24 hours, remove the ice cream from the freezer 15 minutes before you want to serve it. Serve with drizzles of soy cream, maple syrup, a sprinkle of cinnamon and some fruit of your choice.

chocolate mousse with banana cake hearts

preparation: 20 minutes, plus chilling
cooking: 25–30 minutes
serves: 6

Mousse
- 6 oz dairy-free chocolate (70 percent cocoa solids)
- ¼ cup coconut oil
- ¼ cup orange juice
- ¼ cup dark brown sugar
- ½ cup sunflower oil
- ½ cup sweetened soy milk
- ¼ cup medjool dates, pitted and chopped
- 2 tablespoons Cointreau

Banana cake
- 1 banana, mashed
- 1 cup plus 2 tablespoons self-rising wholegrain flour
- ¼ cup rapeseed oil
- ¼ cup soy milk
- ¼ cup agave or maple syrup
- 1 tablespoon chopped glacé cherries
- 1 teaspoon finely grated lemon rind
- 1 teaspoon lemon juice

To decorate
- soy cream
- grated chocolate

Good dairy-free dark chocolate is essential for this recipe.

1 Break the chocolate into pieces, place in a saucepan with the coconut oil, orange juice and sugar, and melt over low heat, stirring constantly.

2 Place the sunflower oil and soy milk in a bowl and combine thoroughly using a handheld mixer. With the mixer still running, gradually add the melted chocolate mixture. Stir in the dates and Cointreau, then chill the mousse in the refrigerator for at least 2 hours.

3 Meanwhile, make the banana cake. Grease an 8-inch cake pan. Preheat the oven to 350°F.

4 Place all the cake ingredients in a bowl and mix thoroughly. Pour the mixture into the prepared cake pan and bake for 20–25 minutes, or until the tip of a sharp knife inserted in the middle of the cake comes out clean.

5 Allow the cake to cool, then use a heart-shaped cookie cutter to cut out 12 shapes from the cake.

6 Whisk the mousse again, then spoon into ramekins or glass dishes. Place a cake heart on top of each one. Drizzle each serving with soy cream and sprinkle with coarsely grated chocolate.

flaming hot peaches with chocolate sauce

preparation: **15** minutes
cooking: **10** minutes
serves: **2**

This dessert is a real show-stopper. The flaming is most impressive if done at the table with the lights down low.

1 Place the cream cheese in a bowl and mash 2 of the strawberries into it.

2 Cut a sliver of flesh from the curved side of each peach half so that they sit level on a plate. Spoon the cream cheese mixture into the hollows of the peaches. Chill in the refrigerator.

3 To make the chocolate sauce, break the chocolate into pieces and melt in a bowl placed over a saucepan of simmering water. (Do not let the bowl touch the water.)

4 Mix in the agave syrup, then add the soy cream or soy milk, a little at a time. Stir in the Cointreau, if using.

5 Decorate the peaches with the grated chocolate and the remaining strawberries, sliced into fans (see page 28, step 3).

6 Heat the whiskey or brandy in a small saucepan on the stove or a bowl in the microwave. When hot, but not boiling, set on fire and carefully pour the flaming liquid over the cold peaches and watch the chocolate melt.

- **2 tablespoons vegan cream cheese (see page 14)**
- **6 strawberries**
- **2 peaches, halved and pitted**
- **1 oz dairy-free dark chocolate (70 percent cocoa solids), coarsely grated or finely chopped**
- **¼ cup whiskey or brandy**

Chocolate sauce
- **3 oz dairy-free dark chocolate (70 percent cocoa solids)**
- **1 tablespoon agave syrup**
- **1 cup soy cream, or ¾ cup sweetened soy milk**
- **1 tablespoon Cointreau (optional)**

black forest chocolate cake

Cake
- 2¼ cups self-rising wholegrain flour
- 1 cup soft brown sugar
- ½ cup rapeseed oil
- ½ cup soy milk
- 2 tablespoons cocoa powder
- 1 tablespoon vegan yogurt (see page 14), bean curd or coconut cream
- 2½ teaspoons cider vinegar
- 2 heaping teaspoons carob powder
- pinch of salt
- 1 oz dairy-free dark chocolate (70 percent cocoa solids)
- fresh cherries or berries, to decorate

Filling
- ¼ cup vegan cream cheese (see page 14)
- 1 teaspoon lime zest
- ¼ cup cherry or blackberry jam

You don't need eggs to make a light-as-air sponge cake. This dairy-free version of a classic gâteau shows you how.

1 Oil two 8-inch circular cake pans and line them with parchment paper. Preheat the oven to 350°F.

2 Place all the cake ingredients except the chocolate in a food processor and beat together thoroughly.

3 Coarsely grate or chop the chocolate and add to the cake mixture. Divide the mixture between the cake pans and level the tops with a spatula.

4 Bake for 25–30 minutes, or until a toothpick inserted into the center of each cake comes out clean. Allow to cool a little, then turn out onto a wire rack to cool completely.

5 Place the cream cheese in a bowl and stir in the lime zest. Spread one side of a cold cake with the lime cream cheese, and spread the other cake with jam. Sandwich together and put on a serving plate.

6 Decorate the cake with fresh cherries or berries and serve with vanilla ice cream and hot chocolate sauce (see page 113) made with Kirsch rather than Cointreau.

mango ice cream

- 2 large mangoes, skinned, pitted and chopped
- 1 banana
- ⅓ cup dried apricots, chopped
- 1 tablespoon lime juice
- 3 tablespoons sunflower oil
- 1 tablespoon flax oil
- 1 tablespoon soy lecithin
- ¼ cup soy milk
- ½ cup essential seed mix (see page 20)

This exotic fruity ice cream is nutritious as well as delicious. It also makes an excellent base for a smoothie (see page 21).

1 Place the mangoes, banana, apricots and lime juice in a blender and mix to a smooth consistency.

2 Combine the oils, soy lecithin and soy milk and whisk well. Add the blended fruit and whisk again. Stir in the seed mix.

3 Transfer the ice-cream mixture to a shallow container with an airtight lid and freeze for 1 hour. Remove from the freezer and break up the mixture with a fork to reduce the ice crystals. Repeat this process every hour for the next 4 hours.

4 Serve the ice cream with berries and coconut cream.

pecan pie

preparation: **15** minutes
cooking: **35** minutes
serves: 6

Pecans were an important food source for native Americans. In recent years, they have been used mostly in ice creams, candies and pastries, such as this one. The addition of molasses adds a rich dark taste and texture, as well as a good helping of calcium, and is balanced by the hint of cinnamon.

1 Preheat the oven to 350°F. Grease a 10-inch pie plate.

2 On a floured surface, roll out the pastry and use it to line the pie plate, trimming off any excess. Arrange parchment paper on top of the pastry, place pie weights on top and bake for 10 minutes.

3 Place the chopped pecans, maple syrup, flour, molasses, carob powder and cinnamon in a bowl and mix well.

4 Heat the soy milk until almost boiling, add the rapeseed oil and mix well using an electric mixer with a whisk attachment. Continue whisking as you add the lime juice.

5 Fold this liquid into the maple syrup mixture, then pour into the pie shell. Arrange the whole pecans on top and bake for 20 minutes.

6 Serve warm with vegan ice cream or soy cream and maple syrup.

- 8 oz vegan shortcrust pastry
- ¾ cup pecans, finely chopped
- ¾ cup maple syrup
- 2 tablespoons self-rising unbleached flour
- 2 tablespoons blackstrap molasses
- 1 teaspoon carob powder
- ½ teaspoon ground cinnamon
- ⅓ cup soy milk
- ⅓ cup rapeseed oil
- 2½ teaspoons lime juice
- ¾ cup whole pecans

peach, apricot and fig crumble with custard

Crumble
- 1 cup plus 2 tablespoons wholegrain flour
- 2 tablespoons rapeseed oil
- 2 tablespoons sweetened soy milk
- ⅓ cup rolled oats
- ¼ cup dark brown sugar
- ¼ cup flaked almonds
- ½ lb peaches, pitted and sliced
- 1½ cups dried apricots, chopped
- 6 fresh or dried figs, diced
- juice of 1 lime
- 1 teaspoon ground cinnamon
- ¼ teaspoon ground nutmeg

Custard
- 2 tablespoons custard powder or cornstarch
- 3 tablespoons maple syrup
- 2 cups oat milk or soy milk

Crumbles are comfort food, best eaten with custard, but are also delicious with ice cream or soy cream. The fruit content can be varied in any way you like: try plum and ginger, strawberry and mango, pear and dried plums, apple and raspberry, or banana, pineapple and coconut.

1 Preheat the oven to 350°F. Pour the flour into a large bowl and lightly mix in the oil and the soy milk with a fork until the mixture forms coarse crumbs. Stir the oats, sugar and flaked almonds into the mixture.

2 Place the fruit in a 1-quart ovenproof dish and sprinkle it with about ¼ cup water, the lime juice, cinnamon and nutmeg.

3 Spoon the crumble mixture over the fruit and bake for 25–30 minutes, until golden brown.

4 Put the custard powder in a bowl, add the maple syrup and ¼ cup of the oat milk and mix well.

5 Heat the remaining milk in a small saucepan until hot but not boiling, then remove from the heat and gradually stir in the custard powder mixture to thicken. Return the pan to medium heat and cook for a few minutes, stirring constantly.

6 Serve the crumble with the hot custard.

- 1 cup dried apricots, chopped
- 1 oz dried papaya, chopped
- 1½ cups sweetened soy milk
- 2 tablespoons flax oil
- 6 strawberries or 1 kiwi fruit, to
  decorate
- coconut cream, to serve

apricot and papaya cream

A light and luscious dessert, much healthier than the non-vegan version, which has a lot of whipped cream.

1 Soak the dried apricots and papaya in the soya milk overnight.

2 Transfer the dried fruit and soy milk to a food processor or blender and mix to a smooth consistency. Add the oil and blend again.

3 Divide the mixture between 6 small glass dishes, then refrigerate until set.

4 Decorate each serving with a sliced strawberry fan (see page 28, step 3) or some slivers of kiwi fruit. Serve with coconut cream.

crème caramel

preparation: 10 minutes, plus chilling
cooking: 25 minutes
serves: 6

The classic French recipe for this dessert is totally dependent on dairy produce. This version tastes equally good with none at all.

1 Thoroughly grease six 3¼-inch ovenproof ramekins. Preheat the oven to 350°F.

2 Stir the sugar into the soy milk, then heat until hot but not boiling. Transfer to a food processor or blender. Add the oil and mix well. Keep the machine running as you add 1 tablespoon of the lime juice and the vanilla extract. The mixture will thicken slightly.

3 Add the cornstarch and mix again. Add the molasses and the remaining lime juice and mix once more. Divide the mixture between the ramekins, place on a baking tray and bake for 25 minutes.

4 Allow to cool, then refrigerate for 2 hours.

5 To serve, stand the ramekins in hot water for a few minutes, then carefully run a very sharp, thin knife around the edges. Turn out onto small plates, drizzle with a little molasses and decorate with strawberries dusted with confectioner's sugar.

- 4 heaping tablespoons confectioner's sugar
- 1 cup sweetened soy milk
- 1 cup rapeseed oil
- 2 tablespoons lime juice
- 2 teaspoons vanilla extract
- 2 scant tablespoons cornstarch
- 5 tablespoons blackstrap molasses, plus extra for drizzling

To decorate
- strawberries
- confectioner's sugar

preparation: 30 minutes, plus chilling
cooking: 45 minutes
serves: 6

date toffee and quinoa custard pie

Pastry base
- 1⅓ cups rye flour
- ¼ cup soy milk
- 2 tablespoons rapeseed oil
- 1 teaspoon linseeds
- 1 teaspoon brown sugar
- 1 teaspoon lime juice
- pinch of carob powder
- pinch of cinnamon

Quinoa custard and coconut cream
- 1 cup plus 2 tablespoons quinoa seeds, flakes or flour
- 1½ cups rice milk
- 2 cups soy milk
- ½ cup maple syrup
- 2 tablespoons sunflower oil
- 1 teaspoon instant decaffeinated coffee
- pinch of salt
- 1 tablespoon lemon juice
- 1 cup coconut milk
- 1 teaspoon vanilla extract
- ½ cup rapeseed oil

Date toffee
- ¼ cup dates, finely chopped
- ¾ cup soy milk
- 2 tablespoons coconut oil
- 2 teaspoons brown sugar
- 1 teaspoon blackstrap molasses
- 1 teaspoon lemon juice
- 2 bananas, sliced

1 Grease an 8-inch tart pan. Preheat the oven to 350°F. Soak the dates for the toffee in the soy milk.

2 Mix together all the pastry ingredients, then roll out on a floured surface and use to line the prepared tart pan. Prick the pastry all over with a fork, then bake for 20–25 minutes until lightly browned. Set aside to cool.

3 Meanwhile, make the custard. Place the quinoa and rice milk in a small saucepan, bring to a boil, then simmer gently for 15 minutes. Add 1½ cups of the soy milk and beat well with an electric mixer or handheld blender. Simmer for another 5 minutes. Add the maple syrup, then divide the mixture equally between 2 bowls. To one add the sunflower oil, coffee, salt and 1 teaspoon of the lemon juice. Mix thoroughly until smooth.

4 To make the coconut cream, heat the remaining soya ½ cup milk and, while still beating, add the remaining lemon juice. Add this liquid to the quinoa mixture without coffee, then add the coconut milk, vanilla extract and rapeseed oil and beat until smooth.

5 Now make the date toffee. Melt the coconut oil (if necessary), then place in a food processor or blender and add the dates and any remaining soy milk, sugar and molasses and blend until smooth and creamy. Add the lemon juice and blend again. Spread the date toffee in the pastry shell, then cover with a layer of sliced banana.

6 Spread the quinoa and coffee mixture on the top and chill for 2 hours. Serve cold with the coconut cream and a dusting of cocoa powder, if you like.

chocolate chip cookies

- coconut oil, for greasing
- 1 cup plus 2 tablespoons self-rising wholegrain flour or unbleached flour plus 1 teaspoon baking powder
- ¼ cup soft brown sugar
- ¼ cup finely chopped dates
- 4 teaspoons carob powder
- 1 teaspoon cinnamon
- pinch of salt
- ½ cup sweetened soy milk
- ⅓ cup rapeseed oil
- 1 teaspoon vanilla extract
- 1 teaspoon finely grated orange zest
- 1 oz dairy-free chocolate or carob, coarsely grated or chopped

Great for a snack at any time, these cookies also go well with ice cream. For a special treat, serve them with a bowl of chocolate sauce (see page 113) for dipping.

1 Line a baking sheet with parchment paper and grease with coconut oil. Preheat the oven to 350°F.

2 Place the flour, sugar, dates, carob powder, cinnamon and salt in a bowl and mix well. Add the milk, oil and vanilla extract and beat with an electric mixer or fork. Stir in the orange zest and grated chocolate.

3 Place 12 spoonfuls of the mixture on the prepared baking sheet and smooth the tops with a wet knife.

4 Bake the cookies for 10 minutes, then cool on a wire rack. Store in an airtight container until needed.

sticky pudding with quinoa coconut ice cream

preparation: 15 minutes, plus freezing
cooking: 1 hour
serves: 6

1 First make the ice cream. Place the rice milk and quinoa in a saucepan, bring to a boil, then simmer gently for 15 minutes. Add the soy milk and beat with an electric mixer or blender. Simmer for another 5 minutes. Add the coconut milk and agave syrup and beat again.

2 Still beating, add the rapeseed oil, then the lemon juice and the vanilla extract. Add the banana and beat until the mixture is smooth. Transfer the mixture to a shallow container with an airtight lid and freeze for 12 hours, stirring every hour or two with a fork to break up any ice crystals.

3 Now make the sticky pudding. Preheat the oven to 350°F. Put the apple juice and plums in a small saucepan and simmer for about 5 minutes, until soft. Add the orange juice, molasses and avocado oil and mix until smooth, using a handheld mixer or blender.

4 Place the flour, soy milk, sugar, lemon juice, orange zest, cinnamon and ginger in a bowl and mix until smooth. Stir in the chopped coconut oil.

5 Place 1 spoon of plum mixture in each of six 3¼ inch ovenproof ramekins and top with 2 spoonfuls of cake mixture. Cover each ramekin with a piece of greased parchment paper and fasten in place with a rubber band. Place the ramekins in a deep roasting pan and pour in boiling water to reach about halfway up the dishes and bake for 35–40 minutes.

6 Run the blade of a sharp knife around the edge of each ramekin to loosen the puddings, then turn them out onto plates and decorate, if you wish, with slices of mango or peach. Serve with the ice cream.

Quinoa coconut ice cream
- ¾ cup rice milk
- ⅔ cup quinoa seeds, flakes or flour
- ¾ cup soy milk
- 1 cup coconut milk
- ¼ cup agave or maple syrup
- ½ cup rapeseed oil
- 1 tablespoon lemon juice
- 1 teaspoon vanilla extract
- 1 banana, chopped

Sticky pudding
- 1 cup apple juice
- ½ cup dried plums
- juice of 1 orange
- 2 tablespoons blackstrap molasses
- 1 tablespoon avocado oil
- 1½ cups self-rising flour
- ¾ cup soy milk
- 1 tablespoon soft brown sugar
- 2½ teaspoons lemon juice
- 1 teaspoon finely grated orange zest
- ½ teaspoon cinnamon
- ½ teaspoon fresh ginger, peeled and finely chopped
- ¼ cup chilled and solidified coconut oil, chopped

index

index

acknowledgments

Executive Editor Nicola Hill

Executive Art Editor Joanna MacGregor

Designer Bill Mason

Special Photography Clive Bozzard-Hill

Picture Librarian Jennifer Veall

Production Controller Martin Croshaw

Photography **Octopus Publishing Group Limited**/Clive Bozzard-Hill 3, 5, 13, 19, 23, 27, 31, 35, 37, 39, 43, 45, 49, 53, 57, 61, 65, 69, 73, 77, 81, 85, 87, 89, 93, 97, 99, 103, 105, 107, 111, 115, 119, 123/Stephen Conroy 8 top left/William Reavell 7, 8 bottom right